RECRUITING

With a

CLEAN SOUL

Because: "Sell it, fill it, bill it" is so last decade.

ZANDY HOUGHTON

Copyright © 2026 by Zandrea Houghton

All rights reserved.

No part of this book may be copied, stored, or shared in any form without permission from the author or publisher, except for brief quotations used in reviews or commentary.

First published in Great Britain by Clean Soul Publishing
Birmingham, United Kingdom

ISBN (Paperback): 978-1-9192505-0-2
ISBN (eBook): 978-1-9192505 -1-9
This book is based on real experiences in the recruitment industry. Some names, roles, and organisations have been adjusted to protect privacy, but the lessons, humour, and truth remain intact.

Book Cover by Christopher Barber

Illustrations by Zandrea Houghton

First edition 2026

Dedications

To the recruiter who once made me feel she was doing me a favour, then pushed me to the brink of desperation.

You taught me everything recruitment shouldn't be about.

And lit the fire to prove it could be done better.

Contents

Introduction

I'm willing to bet that right now, you've got your head in your hands.

Maybe you've been ghosted by clients, countered by candidates, or handed a job description that turned out to be more fiction than fact.

Your to-do list reads like a game of recruitment bingo:
Lies? Check.
Let-downs? Check.
Back to the drawing board? Bingo.

No matter how hard you work, the results just aren't coming like they used to.

I get it. You're tired of recruitment feeling like a soul-crushing grind. You're not alone. The challenges are real, and disillusionment in our industry is at an all-time high. If recruitment had a relationship status, it would probably be "It's complicated."

If any of this feels familiar, it doesn't mean you've been doing recruitment wrong. It means you've been doing it exactly how you were taught.

Most of us inherited a system that rewarded speed, activity, and persuasion because, for a long time, it worked. When it stopped working, the training didn't change; the pressure just increased.

Is Our Industry Doomed?

It's no surprise that many of us are wondering whether recruitment is broken.

Hiring is in a state of flux. There's a growing disconnect between supply and demand: fewer jobs, applicant-heavy yet candidate-light markets, political and economic pressure, generational shifts, expectation gaps between clients and candidates, and the looming impact of AI. Small wonder it feels like we're heading for the knacker's yard.

However, there is no escaping the fact that companies will always need help finding talent, and talent will always need help finding the right career path. At our core, we are expert market navigators, connecting value with opportunity faster, smarter, and with better long-term outcomes than either party could achieve alone.

> Recruitment isn't broken.
> It's our application within it, that is seriously flawed

The Outdated Recruitment Playbook

That flawed application has a root cause: the sell-it, fill-it, bill-it blueprint forged during recruitment's heyday.

It's become so ingrained in our culture that we don't even question it. We just call it 'recruitment.

This wasn't just a set of tools; it was a belief system.

Do the activity, crank the numbers. The results will follow. Dials made. CVs sent. Interviews booked. Quantity equals success.

Or so we were told.

The quality of those conversations, and the long-term outcomes, mattered far less than keeping the scoreboard moving.

We were also encouraged to rely on persuasion and manipulation to get deals over the line. Convince candidates to take jobs that weren't right. Win business by promising what couldn't realistically be delivered. Push candidates into roles that didn't fit, just to keep the pipeline flowing.

And now we're teaching AI to do the same thing, faster, louder, and at an industrial scale: spray CVs wider. Push candidates harder. Spam the market into submission. It's the same broken playbook, just automated.

Those of us at the sharp end of recruitment can see that it no longer works. The market isn't buying it. Clients don't trust us. Candidates don't trust us, and if we're being really honest, we've stopped trusting them, too.

> *If we work in a people-centric industry that's utterly devoid of trust, then maybe it's time we gave our heads a wobble.*

The Alternative

Despite everything, I know most recruiters want to do this job well.

I can see you calling out dodgy practices, offering prayers to the LinkedIn algorithm, sharing insights, and genuinely trying to help candidates, clients, and one another. The desire to provide a valued and respected recruitment service is still very much alive.

So here we are, caught between a rock and a hard place.

We know the old ways won't take us forward, and AI won't save us; it'll just scale the mess.

There is another option, and you're holding it in your hands.

This book introduces a clear, practical methodology for recruiting that works with people, not against them, and aligns with your values and the way you want to work.

It's built on three core principles that underpin every recruitment conversation, whether you realise it or not. Apply them consistently, and what happens on the desk, and over the life of a hire, fundamentally changes.

When applied properly, this approach helps you surface the truth earlier, make better decisions with less friction, and build commitment without pressure by creating the conditions where trust can actually form.

You'll see how to rebuild that trust from the inside out, with candidates who feel processed, clients who've been burned, and an industry that's been stuck defending itself for far too long.

And just so you know, the legacy playbook isn't going anywhere. It'll be sat firmly on the naughty step for the duration of this book, where we'll be calling it out, challenging it, and occasionally ripping the living piss out of it. By the end, we'll be ready to kick it into touch once and for all.

When You Apply the Principles in This Book, You'll Notice:

- Higher levels of engagement and responsiveness from clients, candidates, and prospects
- More accurate forecasts and pipelines that won't make your manager's head explode in weekly meetings
- Fewer objections, rejections, and "back to the drawing board" moments
- Freedom from high-pressure, manipulative sales tactics; your market will start closing you
- The ability to focus only on assignments that are genuinely commercially viable
- Your sanity will improve

And the best part?

This methodology works.
Regardless of your personality type, yes, even if you're an introvert who considers "networking" a dirty word.
Regardless of what's happening in the wider market.
Within the structure you're already working in.

Most importantly, you already know how to do this.

This isn't about changing who you are. It's about unlocking what's already there, the part of you that wants to be the recruiter who actually gives a toss.

Reputation Matters

Ten Ways we are Losing Oxygen

We haven't damaged our reputation by one scandal, one platform, AI, or a few dodgy recruiters.

It has been shaped in the everyday, nitty-gritty behaviours that have become so normal we barely notice them anymore.

1. Treating People like Inventory

When candidates become "stock" and jobs become "units", humanity leaves the building. People can tell when they are being processed rather than understood.

2. Asking Basic Type Questions

"Talk me through your CV."
"Why are you looking?"
"Do you use agencies?"

That's not consulting. It's going through a list and produces predictable, shallow answers. Then we wonder why they lie to us?

3. Over-Selling Roles we do not Understand

Promising "career-defining opportunities" without understanding the job, the manager, the internal politics, or the reality. The fallout lands on the candidate.

4. Ghosting, then Wondering Why Candidates Do not Trust us

Nothing erodes credibility faster than silence, especially after you initiated contact. You cannot complain about candidate behaviour if you model the worst of it.

5. Confusing Confidence with Competence

"I've filled loads like this before" energy masquerading as expertise. Assumptions dressed up as certainty are still assumptions.

6. Prioritising Speed over Suitability

Rushing to submit someone rather than the right someone creates short-term wins and long-term damage. Bad hires linger far longer than your invoice.

7. Using Pressure Instead of Perspective

Manufactured urgency. Emotional nudging. "Other candidates are further along."
If a decision needs manipulation, it probably shouldn't happen at all.

8. Hiding Behind Process Instead of Owning Judgement

"It's the client's decision." "It's company policy." "It's how the system works."

Process is not a personality, and it is certainly not an excuse.

9. Calling Out the Market and Demanding it Behaves Better

Publicly scolding candidates, applicants, hiring managers, gatekeepers, or "the market" for not behaving as we would like is reputation suicide.

Posts that translate as: “Candidates should stop ghosting.” “Hiring managers need to be more decisive.” “People need to respect recruiters more.” “The market has lost all professionalism.”

These posts do not elevate the profession. They expose frustration, entitlement, and a fundamental misunderstanding of power dynamics.

Markets do not respond to demands. People do not change their behaviour because they have been told off publicly.

When recruiters lecture the very people they rely on, they position themselves as victims rather than professionals and confirm every negative stereotype the industry already carries.

Influence is built through understanding behaviour, not shaming it.

10. Measuring Success by Fees Alone

When revenue is the only scoreboard, behaviour follows. Trust, outcomes, experience, and reputation do not fit neatly into a KPI, so they get ignored until the industry wonders why no one likes us.

Why We Don’t Acknowledge the Damage

If you recognised yourself in that list, it’s not an accusation. We’ve been taught and encouraged to operate this way. It is evidence of how normalised these behaviours have become.

We all know the reputational rot is there. A blind man up a dark alley could see it. The scepticism, the guarded responses, the quiet disengagement that appears the moment we say what we do. None of this is subtle or new. And yet, despite recognising it, we do not act on it.

That is because reputational damage is easy to rationalise away when you are operating in the thick of day-to-day desk life. We are focused on outcomes. Filling roles. Managing fallout. Keeping revenue moving. Reputation does not sit neatly on a to-do list, and it rarely presents itself as an urgent, isolated problem demanding immediate action.

So instead of addressing it collectively, we internalise it individually.

We tell ourselves that if we do good work, act with integrity, show empathy, and build strong personal relationships, we will be fine. We invest in our personal brands, our positioning, and our standards. We also kid ourselves that it automatically differentiates from the recruiters who don't, and this means more business for us.

Psychologically, this makes sense. Thinking in silos allows us to believe we are standing apart from the behaviour that causes the damage in the first place. It reassures us that while the industry may have a problem, we are not the problem, and therefore the consequences will not really touch us.

I often hear, "All industries have good and bad in them."

That is a very comforting belief. It is also deeply misleading.

Reputation does not operate at the level of individual intent. It operates at the level of collective experience. Markets do not neatly separate "good recruiters" from "bad recruiters" when forming opinions. They respond to patterns. Repeated interactions that feel transactional, frustrating, or opaque are generalised.

You cannot brand yourself out of a damaged reputation. You cannot personally opt out of a collective problem that everyone else has learned to tolerate.

The Cost of Inaction

This is not prophecy or a prediction of a random recruiter. It is already happening.

Cost 1: Reach

Response rates are collapsing because they are protecting their time and attention.

Recruiter outreach is increasingly filtered, ignored, or auto-archived, sometimes by people, increasingly by technology acting on their behalf. What once took fifty messages just to get an "*hello*" now takes hundreds.

Same outcome, but more effort.

Cost 2: Margin

As trust erodes, efficiency disappears. Roles take longer to fill, drop-out rates increase, and shortlists stretch. You work harder to deliver the same result while margins erode.

This is the Trust Tax. Every time one of the 10 behaviours is repeated, the tax rises for everyone.

Cost 3: Relevance

Hiring managers are being sold a simple story. Fewer recruiters. Lower fees. More technology.

Whether those solutions actually work is almost irrelevant. Once recruiters are positioned as optional rather than essential, the damage is done.

Fees are not negotiated down, they are avoided altogether.

The silo you may feel safe operating within eventually becomes an economic prison where you work harder for less.

Why This Book Exists

No one is going to come along and install a good reputation for us next Tuesday.

There is no governing body, platform, or piece of technology waiting in the wings to fix how recruitment is experienced. If anything, many of the solutions currently being sold are designed to work around recruiters, not elevate them.

The responsibility sits where it always has, with the people doing the work.

Reputation is shaped collectively, but it is built in the nitty-gritty of individual desks. In the calls we make. The questions we ask. The assumptions we default to. The pressure we apply. The things we choose to ignore because they feel inconvenient in the moment.

This means the fix does not require grand gestures or wholesale reinvention. It requires hundreds of small, practical changes made consistently by people who care enough about the craft to examine how they actually operate.

This book exists to do exactly that.

Every fix, every alternative, and every practical adjustment explored here is rooted in the reality of day-to-day recruitment. Just the work, done better.

Elevate the reputation collectively, and everyone benefits. Ignore it, and no amount of individual excellence will stop the slow erosion.

When reputation is already wobbling, when response rates are collapsing, when trust is thin, and tech is circling like sharks... trying something more human isn't risky.

Doing nothing is.

When the Monster Came to Town

A "Back in the Day" Parable

Once upon a time, a long time ago, our recruitment forefathers were a rare breed, blessed with a strong work ethic and a deep respect for both industry and candidates.

As time passed, a vast worldwide web was spun, which became known as the Internet.

Soon after, a friendly monster appeared in the world and said to the candidates:

"Let me have your CV, and with the powers I possess, I shall showcase it to the whole world... and I will provide you with the ability to see all the available jobs, and make it easy for you to apply to them. You will not have to pay me for this service, as I will collect the money from the holder of the job".

And the candidates said, "*Sound, I'll have some of that.*" No more buying local newspapers or squinting at the Sits Vac adverts. No more stamps, envelopes, or waiting weeks for a reply.

The friendly monster then went to the recruiters and said:

"For a small fee, you will be able to search for candidates for the jobs you are trying to fill, and with the powers I have, you will be able to showcase your vacancies to all the candidates in the world".

And the recruiters said, "*Sound, bring it on,*" as they no longer had to practice their dark art by advertising their vacancies in the newspapers, and would have a greater choice of candidates to choose from, which meant they could fill more jobs, more quickly, which would earn them great wealth.

Many recruitment wannabees saw how they too could get rich, so they jumped on a vehicle called a bandwagon and headed for a destination called the "*Recruitment Heyday*."

All was good in the world of recruitment for a few years, anyway, and unfettered by legislation, they filled their boots. But as their bank accounts swelled, so did their egos. With a click of a button, many candidates' CVs could be found, and the service that recruiters once provided became rushed and poorly executed.

Candidates were left to feel like a means to an end, fodder to feed the recruitment fat cats, and they did not like this very much. As a result, they began to lie and let them down and some turned into ghosts.

Hiring managers initially enjoyed the broader choice of candidates, but soon grew weary of paying inflated fees for square pegs in round holes. They grew tired of being told that every recruiter was "the best" and began to lose faith. Many retreated behind HR, PSLs, and gatekeepers. Some turned into ghosts as well.

Recruiters could see that their market share and bank balances were shrinking, and they took to blaming the candidates, the market, their bosses, anyone apart from themselves.

To stand out from their ever-growing competition, they resorted to skulduggery and developed dodgy sales practices.

Before long, dogs were eating dogs, and they were all forced to play an unsavoury game of 'fastest finger first'.

They forgot about the service they should provide to the industry and candidates, and worked only to serve themselves.

Bit by bit, the soul of recruitment faded, its noble roots buried beneath a mountain of shortcuts and empty exchanges.

But all was not lost. For in the shadows of this changing world, a new light began to flicker, one that spoke of trust over targets, integrity over ego, and the return of a clean soul to recruitment.

R.I.P
MONSTER
1999-2025
BELOVED BY:
CV SHIFTERS
FASTEST-FINGER
FIRSTERS
BOOLEAN SEARCH
STRING LOVERS
GONE, BUT NOT
FILTERED

PART ONE

The Three Principles of Recruitment Excellence

The Recruitment Dynamic

A few years ago, I wrote a post called *Recruitment* 2.0, listing all the ways I thought the model was broken. My manager, at the time, disagreed. He said recruitment was working exactly as it was meant to. Bruised ego aside (I'd spent hours crafting that post), I realised he was right.

At its simplest, the model revolves around three core elements: **clients, jobs, and candidates.**

This is what I call the **Recruitment Dynamic**, a phrase you'll come across often in this book. When all three are aligned, the system works; remove one, and nothing moves.

> You have a client but no job?... No fee.
> A job but no candidate?... No fee.
> A candidate, but no job?... Still no fee.

Each element should carry equal weight, but look at how the balance plays out in real life:
Clients become the priority; they are the ones who pay the invoice.
Jobs get reduced to admin.
Candidates are treated like stock to be shifted.

That's where we become our own worst enemy. We built a process that serves one element at the expense of the others, and then act surprised when deals fall apart, candidates vanish, or clients "suddenly" fill the job internally.

We're just busy fools keeping the illusion of progress alive.

On the front cover of this book is an image of a Penrose Triangle, also known as an impossible triangle.

It is an optical illusion where each side appears connected. Its purpose is to challenge our perception of reality.

Each side of the triangle represents one of the three elements of the recruitment dynamic; all are equal and interconnected with each other.

When we embed the three core principles of mindset, relationships, and the way we ask questions into the recruitment dynamic, as a whole, we achieve harmony and alignment.

Each element supports the others, trust replaces tension, and the process moves with ease instead of resistance.

Why Part One Matters

Now that we're two missed quarters away from digging in the dirt for edible roots, the thought leaders, gurus, and once-upon-a-time big billers are out in force, giving us the benefit of their wisdom.

Adopt a resilient mindset:

Don't take rejection personally. Take it on the chin. Every "no" gets you closer to a "yes."
Translation: Double down on the legacy playbook: more activity, more BD, more outreach, twice the rejection and burnout in half the time. The quiet subtext? If you're not operating on persistence, stamina, and grit, you're in the wrong industry. Go hard or go home. When results don't materialise, guess who gets the blame?

Chapter 1 explores a different mindset that aligns with your values, work ethic, and the market as it actually is.

Build stronger relationships with your clients:

Work retained. Niche down. Identify what keeps them awake at night (oh please). Win them round with market expertise, data, and personal brand.
Translation: These are ring-fenced by the select few who've already built and established successful desks. Relationship-building is often viewed as a soft skill where you either possess it or you don't.
Be honest, have you ever had any training on it? The focus is often centred on techniques, objections, and closing skills, rather than how to build relationships.

Chapter 2 clears the fog: what trust looks like in conversation, from the moment you utter those first words.

Push back: ask tougher questions:

Apparently, the answer to a broken system is to interrogate it harder. We're told to "use open questions" and "dig deeper," but rarely shown what better actually sounds like in a live call, or how to avoid sounding like a customs officer.

Chapter 3 illustrates how our traditional questions can hinder the process and lead to ghosting.

Chapter 4 builds the kind of questions that uncover what's true.

Chapter 5 provides a simple framework that guides questioning from initial contact to clear next steps.

Part One isn't another round of hollow, advice, the kind that reads well on LinkedIn but doesn't survive five minutes in the real world. It's about the *how*: the actual questions that cut deeper, the way trust can be built from your very first conversation, and how a shifting mindset underpins everything.

Worked together, these principles don't just sit on top of your process; they are the foundation, the infrastructure of it all, keeping the whole thing alive, with more backbone than the usual industry clichés and something you can actually use, not just nod along to.

Mindset next. Bring coffee.

Trust Pie

Recipe

A real hearty Trust Pie isn't something you can buy from Greggs. It's made, slowly, deliberately, with a fair amount of restraint, and zero sugar-coating

Ingredients

Mindset – a good dollop
This is the base. If it is transactional, impatient, or ego-driven, no amount of technique will save the dish.
Relationships – a good dollop
The binding agent. Without it, the recipe will just crumble, and you'll have fragments of interaction masquerading as progress.
Questions – a good dollop
The depth and flavour. Asked well, they enrich everything. Asked poorly, they overpower or leave a bitter aftertaste.

Each ingredient should be measured in equal parts and be fresh. Do not use outdated ones from the legacy pantry

Method

Start with mindset (the base) and intentionally fold in relationships. Sprinkle in your questions, generously and thoughtfully. Avoid any harsh whisking, as it leads to surface-level rapport, false confidence, ghosting, and a soggy bottom.

Serving Suggestion

Best served over time.
Works equally well with candidates, clients, and when taking on a job.
Results improve dramatically when applied consistently, not selectively.

Important Note

This recipe cannot be rushed, outsourced, or automated.
Anyone promising “trust at scale” is selling reheated leftovers.

Chapter 1
Mindset
The Beat has Changed, So Must We

Just in case you were planning to skip this chapter because you think it's one of those vision-board, manifest-your-dreams-before-breakfast type things, let me reassure you: it has nothing to do with attitude or pretending to be something you're not.

Or maybe you think it's the boring bit, so you're scanning the table of contents for the chapter on objection-handling techniques. Save yourself the bother. There isn't one.

That's not an oversight. When you use this approach, people stop needing to push back. It's prevention, not firefighting.

But since you're already here, you might as well stick with it.

We'll explore why recruitment feels like it's losing the plot, why your desk feels harder to run than it once did, and why all the volume-based activity in the world still isn't delivering what it used to.

If you want to reduce ghosting, build loyalty, increase engagement, and protect your fees, this blueprint will show you how to do it in a way that actually makes sense.

Let's begin.

This isn't about Toughening it Out

You'll hear many people talk about mindset as if it were just a matter of resilience. Be tougher, bounce back, push harder, keep going as if it's a coping mechanism, a shield. This isn't about being able to take more hits. It's about seeing things differently so you stop taking the hits in the first place. Resilience without reflection just keeps you trapped in the same old loop.

Mindset, the way we're talking about it here, isn't about grit. It's about aligning with your market and changing the lens.

Where it all Starts

Mindset is the internal framework that shapes everything you do, whether you're aware of it or not.

It's a collection of beliefs, a mental blueprint formed from your experiences, training, successes, and setbacks. It determines how you interpret the world, how you perceive others, and what you decide matters most in any given moment.

It determines how you present yourself at your desk every morning, how you respond when someone ghosts you, whether you listen or just wait to speak, whether you chase or connect, and whose needs you're trying to meet, yours or theirs.

Most people assume their mindset is reality. But it isn't. It's a filter, and if that filter is outdated, then your reactions, decisions, and strategy will be too. If the beliefs running your desk are misaligned with how your market thinks, you're always going to feel like you're swimming upstream.

What happens is not the problem.
What you believe about it determines how you respond.
Your response, repeated over time, becomes your reputation.

The Macarena Mindset

Many of us are still showing up to the recruitment dance floor as if it were 1999. We are the recruitment equivalent of the drunk uncle at a wedding doing the Macarena long after the DJs switched to house music. We're sweating, pointing, convinced we're smashing it. Same moves, same mindset, same blind hope that if we just turn up the volume, the market will start dancing with us again.

Take the seasoned recruiter: they've built a career on graft, targets, and a no-nonsense belief that the harder you push, the more you'll place. That belief system has been reinforced over time by success, recognition, and the promise that volume equals victory. So, when the market shifts and that same approach stops working, they don't question the mindset; they question the market.

Then there's the rookie: dropped into the middle of this legacy rave, handed a headset full of cold call advice and KPI dashboards, and told, "Just do what we've always done." So they do, and when it doesn't work, they assume they're the problem, that they're not good enough, that they're not cut out for recruitment. We lose good potential because they've inherited a mindset built for a different era.

Many of them don't even realise what's going wrong. They think it's their confidence, their voice, their pitch, anything but the outdated playbook glued to their hand. So they keep grinding, convinced they're one more "motivational coffee" away from cracking it, when really the method itself is the issue. If anything needs retraining, it's the industry, not the rookies.

This is about waking up to a market that no longer thinks the way we think they do. The people we serve are making decisions very differently now.

Let's break it down:

How we Sell vs How they Buy

We're Still Trying To...	They Are Trying To...
Sell a 'fantastic opportunity'	See if it aligns with their values.
Ask Tick-box Questions on (salary, location and notice periods)	Explore meaning, growth, flexibility and well-being.
Get the job on as fast as possible.	Diagnose if the job is even the right 'fix' for them
Sell process (screening, shortlisting, interviewing)	Buy outcome (reduced failure, cost, culture fit and brand protection)
Win on fee % or rebate terms.	Access total ROI, long-term partnership and trustworthiness

To quote the words of an infamous didgeridoo player and artist: "*Can you see what it is yet?*"

The higher echelons among us might call it an incongruence, a misalignment, or a strategic disconnect.

But for you, me, and the majority:

They ain't buying the way we are selling.

The market is telling us how they buy, but not in a neatly worded email. They are reacting in silence: ghosting, last-minute bailouts, and pushback.

If we're still using a mindset trained for speed, manipulation, and persuasion, we'll continue to misfire. The calls won't convert, the CVs won't stick, the trust won't land.

So what do we do? Keep blaming the market? Bang out educational LinkedIn posts, hoping clients and candidates will recognise how they can get a much better service from us if they behave in a certain way? Should we continue to expect them to conform to our way of selling?

Surely if we seek to understand more about how they buy into our services, it makes sense to adapt our narrative to align with theirs?

The onus is on us to do that because they don't need 'educating'; they just need to be understood.

What's stopping us?

Deep down we know the market's changed. We know our efforts are not landing as well as they used to, and yet we keep pressing play.
It's not that we don't see it; it's that we keep hoping we won't have to change. So we stick with what's familiar, even when it's failing us.

So if it's not ignorance, a lack of awareness, or effort, what is it?

Ego: The Uninvited Desk Mate

We all operate under a sense of self. It's part of our make-up, hardwired, inherited, inevitable. It's the part of us that wants to be respected and valued, believing that our work matters, even when our desks are as dry as a Ryvita in August.

When we've grafted, built reputations, survived KPIs, led teams, dodged backdoor fees, and stayed (mostly) sane, we defend it: loudly, proudly, and sometimes irrationally.

If we admit the old way isn't working, we're not just questioning the method; we're questioning ourselves, and that's not exactly the stuff of inspirational wall art.

We've been conditioned to operate from ego. Ego says, "*I need to control this.*" It whispers, "*If I don't lead the conversation, I lose.*"

When things get tough, we default to activity: making more calls, sending more CVs, generating more noise, anything to drown out the panic.

We were trained to sell in this manner, but we were never taught how to help them buy.

It's our ego and pride that stop us from looking in the mirror and asking:

"*What if I'm part of the reason the market doesn't trust us?*"
"*What if we taught candidates to ghost us... by treating them like a means to an end?*"

So we protect our methods, our back catalogue of wins, and that final shred of smugness that says, "*I remember when this used to work.*"

We continue to buy into the old ways because it feels safer than admitting it's broken.

It's not arrogance, cockiness, or swagger; it's just good old-fashioned recruiter pride, layered with a heavy dose of "*if it ain't broke*" denial.

So maybe we should look at fixing this.

Enter the Clean Soul Mindset

So far in this chapter, we've uncovered the old-school ways still running the show, the way we sell that doesn't match how our market buys, and the quiet sabotage that ego and pride sneak into the mix. So now it's time to step out of the echo chamber.

It boils down to two words:

THEM-FIRST

That's it. That's the magic. You can close the book now. (But please don't, I've got a few more uncomfortable truths coming your way.)

Them-First isn't about people-pleasing or rolling over. It's a strategy rooted in relevance and alignment, because when you show up curious, present, and focused on them, not your outcome, everything changes.

Suddenly, conversations feel different. Candidates open up, clients listen, trust builds and the relationship takes hold. You stop chasing and start connecting.

But to get there, you've got to climb out of the "*What's In It For Me*" loop. This runs quietly behind the scenes on every call, every nudge, every speculative CV sent.

Of course, we want to help our market, but we also want the placement, the fee, and the hit that proves we're still nailing it. This is where it all starts to unravel because our market can smell it. They know when we're serving ourselves and when we're genuinely trying to help. They may not be able to put it into words, but they feel it, and the moment they do, the dynamic changes.

However, when you come from a 'Them-First' mindset, they sense that too. The tone softens, trust builds and the relationship takes hold. It's a subtle shift, but it changes everything.

The Commercial Realities

A them-first mindset isn't about ignoring that we still have targets to meet, calls to make, interviews to book, ratios to track, and KPIs to justify. We still need to bill. We still have to do all of that because, unfortunately, nobody's paying us in LinkedIn likes.

But...

When you stop seeing every conversation as a transaction
When you stop reducing people to CVs and clients to job specs
When you stop viewing your day as a spreadsheet to be survived...

Everything shifts. The calls become less forced. The outreach is less awkward. The pipeline is less punishing. Suddenly, the metrics start to matter because they reflect momentum, authentic engagement, conversations, and progress.

You'll still be working just as hard, but it won't feel as heavy. That's when you start to enjoy it again. Even on a Monday. Even when your CRM has frozen for the third time.

Actionable Shifts: How to Build a Clean Soul Mindset

Become a Servant:
Recruitment is a service. We serve; therefore, we are servants. But when success became the driving force, we got greedy. We only helped when it benefited us. We only served ourselves.

You don't need to grab a mop or break into a rendition of "It's a Hard-Knock Life," but maybe, just maybe, stop opening every call with what you want.

Serve first. Ask second. Sell last.

Listen to Your Market:
They're speaking. Loudly. They speak through silence, ghosting, last-minute dropouts, and carefully worded brush-offs. Your job is to decode it. Ask better questions, read trends, understand the climate, and grasp the dynamics of different generations. Understand the pressure they are under, even if they haven't told you yet.

And then, for the love of recruitment, act on it.

Balance the Bias:
We hold candidates to standards we rarely expect from clients. We expect punctuality, honesty, feedback, communication, and flexibility. But when a client ghosts us for three weeks or cancels interviews with zero notice? We say nothing, stay polite, and work harder to keep them on side. That's bias, and our market is aware of it.
We forgive the client's silence but judge the candidate's delay.
We over-service one and get frustrated with the other. If we're going to serve both sides, we've got to stop playing favourites. Hold both to the same level of accountability and empathy.

It's about building trust with all elements of the recruitment dynamic not just the one that might send you a brief.

Utilise Your Snack Drawer:
You know the one. Dusty biscuits. That granola bar you're not going to eat, and right at the back, a half-crushed folder from that time management training you had three years ago, which hasn't seen the light of day since.

Now's the moment.

Slide your ego, your "*what's in it for me*" agenda, and your old-school pride under the flapjack.
Your market doesn't give a rat's arse about your targets, KPIs, and desperation.

How It Will Feel

At first? Unnatural. A bit like switching to a standing desk after years of being glued to a chair. Your legs will ache. You'll feel exposed, and you will question every life choice that brought you to this moment. You may even be tempted to sit back down again. But then you notice that your posture improves, your back doesn't ache so much, and you have a smug sense of superiority over your chair-bound colleagues.

You will feel more like you. The real you.

A Final Word (and an Apology)

If, by this point, you've developed an uncontrollable urge to do the Macarena, I'm sorry. Genuinely.
There's nothing worse than a '90s wedding dance track you didn't ask for, stuck on loop in your head while trying to do serious work.

And just when you thought it couldn't get any worse... I went and replaced it with *Tie Me Kangaroo Down, Sport.*

You're welcome.

Relationships next: Bring herbal tea.

Mindset Rap-up

Them First or Game Over

Yo, you still rocking like it's 1999,
Pitchin' CVs like they're pure goldmine.
Market's changed, it ain't feelin' that beat,
You Macarena'd yourself clean off your seat.

Legacy ego, stuck on a loop,
KPI talk in the WhatsApp group.
Don't freak out, just change your lane,
Stop spinnin' calls like a runaway train.

Put the market first, that's the start,
Not your fee, your funnel, or your LinkedIn chart.
Two words only, Them First, enough said,
Let that live rent-free in your head.

So, slam that drawer with your ego inside,
And let the **Clean Soul** be your north-side guide

Chapter 2
Relationships
"Trust Me, I'm a Recruiter"

Long before AI could spit out job ads or bots could chase leads before your kettle boiled, I learned something that stuck.

It was the mid-90s when we worshipped the flip chart, swore by overhead projectors, and thought a laminated presentation was the height of innovation. I worked for Yellow Pages. They were big on corporate culture, process, and in-depth sales training. We were taught that if you said the right things in the correct order, the sale would follow. Logic in, money out. That was the formula.

I sat next to this girl: quiet, unassuming, no razzle-dazzle or sales swagger. Yet she kept people on the phone longer than anyone else. They warmed to her, they talked, and they came back. While the rest of us wore rejection like an office badge of honour, she racked up awards as if it were nothing. Naturally, I thought she had better data. Maybe luck. I tried to copy her style, but I couldn't crack it. Years went by, and I still didn't know what her secret was.

It wasn't until I moved into recruitment that the penny dropped.

Everyone warned me this industry was cut-throat, but I had this vision of rising above that approach, and my vow was to treat my candidates much better than recruiters had treated me.

So I set a private rule for myself. Every call, with a candidate, a prospect, or a client, had one objective: to establish a genuine relationship and spark trust. Targets still mattered, but while I was on that call, the focus wasn't me; it was them.

That's when it clicked. Her "secret" wasn't a technique at all. It was an intention. She created an environment where people felt safe enough to be honest. No bracing themselves against a sales onslaught. Because of that, they opened up and revealed far more than I had bargained for.

Almost immediately, my rejection levels dropped, and that moment rewired me. It showed me that genuine relationships don't depend on personality, perfect timing, or polished lines. They depend on how you show up.

Fast-forward to today, and that lesson has only grown louder.

Everything in recruitment is relationship based.
Relationships in recruitment are
EVERTHING

When the Middleman is a Machine

AI is now intruding: chatting with candidates, "nurturing" client leads, screening CVs, and sometimes making the initial contact... all without a single human in sight.

The promise? Efficiency, speed, and scale.

The price? Depth and genuine connection.

Because if your tech is handling the first impression, and you only show up after the market has already formed a view of "you", what does that do to trust?

Genuine relationships, the kind that reveal hidden challenges, inspire trust, and change outcomes, aren't built through automation. They're built through understanding and listening.

Being human might not scale like software, but it sticks. It gets remembered, shared, and chosen again and again.

Relationship Myths

Before we discuss building stronger relationships across the recruitment dynamic, let's examine some of the myths that have quietly shaped how we present ourselves to our market.

Myth #1: The Client/Candidate Bias

I get it; the client holds the purse strings and ultimately makes the hiring decisions. So we go out of our way to get in their good books. We remember their dog's name, swamp them with cakes and goodies, and pretend to like their football team (even when it goes against everything we stand for). We do whatever it takes to win them over and earn their trust.

But do we extend the same effort to candidates? Or are they quietly relegated to the "necessary part of the process"?

When we prioritise clients and prospects disproportionately over candidates, we are like a wedding planner who books the perfect venue, arranges the flowers, builds a spectacular cake, and forgets to invite the bride.

Yes. The one person it won't work without.

Reality: Recruitment only works when the balance is right across the recruitment dynamic. Ignoring one of these parts throws everything out of alignment. It's like a wobbly, three-legged stool; you can sit on it for a while, but eventually you will end up on your arse.

Candidates are not just a KPI you tick off. They are your brand ambassadors, your reputation, and a gateway to future success. They notice if you treat them as a product, a means to an end, or simply part of a transaction. When you treat them like partners, they remember that, and they spread the word faster than a recruiter can say, "Do you know anyone else who might be looking?"

Myth #2: Relationships Take Time to Build

While it's true that developing a relationship can take time, we often believe that trust is established after we deliver results. Many of us think that's when the relationship truly begins, and that's when we invest more effort into it, because we then have leverage.

But what happens if we don't deliver? What if the candidate accepts a counteroffer, or the client suddenly decides that their cousin Adam would be a better fit?

Does the relationship vanish into thin air, alongside that candidate after their second interview?

Reality: Relationships start the moment you make contact. The other person forms a mental picture of you from your first words, making judgements and assumptions, just as you are about them.

This initial conversation lays the foundation for the relationship to grow. Even if it's bad, it still counts as a relationship. Time, effort, and successful outcomes don't factor in at this stage.

When your primary goal is to build trust from the start, you lay the groundwork for a thriving relationship quickly. It doesn't matter how brief the interaction is; it could last just a few minutes, as long as you leave them with the impression that they experienced the best version of you as a recruiter.

You may only have a few minutes, but that's plenty of time to either make a great impression... or confirm their worst fears about recruiters.

Make it count.

Myth #3: Face-to-Face Is the Only Way to Build Relationships

There's a long-standing belief in recruitment that it's only possible to build a relationship when you're sitting across the table from someone, making solid eye contact, and sipping something vaguely resembling coffee from a company-branded mug.

Yes, in-person meetings are valuable. I highly recommend you do as many as possible, but they're not the only path to connection.

I have been told by senior management that clients are less likely to say no or be rude when you are face to face. This sounds lovely until they smile, nod, and agree to everything, only to change their mind when you leave.

So what exactly did you build? A relationship? Or just a temporary performance under fluorescent lighting?

Reality: Typically, your first contact will be over the phone. That's not a limitation; it's your chance to initiate a relationship without the distractions of travel time, car park scrambles, and awkward biscuit negotiations.

When the intention is right, relationships don't depend on geography; they depend on how we made them feel.

Myth #4: You Need a Winning Personality

There's a myth that to be successful in recruitment, you need to be a particular type: funny, charming, charismatic, a bit of a social butterfly with a good handshake and a killer pout for your LinkedIn profile picture.

Yes, being friendly helps, but relying solely on personality? That's a risky game. There's always someone out there who's more polished, more charming, or has a better camera angle.

Reality: You don't need to be universally liked. You just need to be real.

People aren't buying your jokes or charm; they're buying how you can help them solve their problems. The real currency is value, not the volume of emojis.

The goal isn't to make them like you. The objective is for you to like them, to be genuinely interested, curious, and engaged in what matters to them. That's where connection happens.

You give others permission to do the same when you show up as yourself, without trying to impress, outperform, or over-polish. That's when trust is built. That's when relationships stick.

Myth #5: Ask "How Are You?" to Build Rapport

There's a long-standing belief in recruitment that a little small talk is the golden gateway to building a relationship. And the default opener? "Hi, how are you?"

Come on. This phrase is as predictable as a recruiter saying they "thrive in a fast-paced environment." It's polite, automatic, and utterly hollow. You don't know them, they don't know you, and no one's about to open up and rattle off their major life disappointments to a stranger on a first call.

So what do you get?

A forced, flat "I'm fine" from someone who is likely busy, stressed, mildly annoyed, or wondering why they answered an unknown number in the first place.

Reality: Saying, "How are you?" doesn't build a relationship; it starts the conversation with a lie. No one is ever just fine.

Hardly the basis for a trusting relationship, is it?

Myth #6: You Have to Be an Industry Expert

There's pressure in recruitment to present yourself as the expert: to wow people with your knowledge, sound polished, prepared, and two steps ahead at all times. Some recruiters feel compelled to open every conversation with a deep dive into market trends, salary benchmarking, competitor insights, and perhaps a PowerPoint presentation for good measure.

When you focus too much on impressing, you stop listening.

You're not building a relationship; you're just broadcasting.

Reality: You don't build trust by showing how much you know; you create it by showing how invested you are in helping them solve their challenges.

Clients and candidates aren't looking to be dazzled; they want to be understood. Being knowledgeable is great (and necessary), but it shouldn't come at the cost of being human. Instead of filling every silence with facts, try creating room for conversation.

Curiosity trumps cleverness every time.

What Do we Do with These Myths?

Reading through those myths might feel like airing recruitment's dirty laundry, and most of us have fallen for at least one of them at some point. While they might seem harmless, they quietly shape how we present ourselves. Worse, they diminish our opportunity to build relationships that actually make a difference.

If we're already picking up the phone to call a client, prospect, or candidate, why wouldn't we approach that moment with the intention of forming a genuine relationship? We're doing the outreach anyway, so why not make it mean something? Instead of thinking, "What can I get from this?", try, "What kind of experience can I leave them with, even if it goes nowhere?"

This is where the myths really trip us up. They train us to rush, pitch, and broadcast instead of connect.

They put us in performance mode, when what people actually respond to is presence; someone who sounds like a human being, not a walking KPI.

Most recruiters aren't short on skill; we're short on permission to slow down long enough to build something real. When you start every interaction with the intention of leaving someone better than when you found them, everything shifts. You're no longer chasing; you're engaging. You're not proving your worth; you're demonstrating it.

When you work like that, you have nothing to lose and everything to gain.

Building Relationships the Clean Soul Way

Get Your Head in the Right Place

Every interaction is a blank canvas. No assumptions, no expectations, no ulterior motives; just a simple objective: to create a relationship.

Forget trying to win, impress, or secure your favoured outcome. The second you make building a relationship your primary objective, rather than filling a job or hitting a KPI, you'll notice a shift in how people respond. They sense the difference, open up, and stop seeing you as just another recruiter.

This is where relationships stop being a technique and start becoming your advantage.

Rapport vs Relationships

Rapport is fine. It's nice. It's warm. The polite smile at the start of the call. The "How was your weekend?" that buys you a moment to breathe.

However, rapport does not necessarily equate to a relationship. If your intention to build a relationship is there, rapport naturally follows.

Rapport is fluff. A relationship is leverage.

Rapport is surface-level. A relationship is a business advantage.

One smooths the way; the other builds the bridge.

Take Responsibility

Every so often, we get lucky. We call someone cold, and the conversation just clicks. There's chemistry, flow, and a bit of banter. It feels effortless, like you've known them for ages. They are instant. I call these random relationships; unfortunately, they don't happen very often.

As recruiters, we cannot afford to wait for these to happen. It is our responsibility, our job, to get on their wavelength and create the relationship deliberately, thoughtfully, and with intention.

When you strip back all the myths, you will find no real difference between a business relationship and a personal one. The context may change, but the fundamentals remain the same. Whether it's your best friend or a hiring manager you cold-called this morning, the same building blocks apply: trust, honesty, integrity, good listening, and mutual respect.

Even the briefest exchange can leave a lasting impression when we approach conversations with presence and purpose. So take ownership of the tone, quality, and outcome of every interaction. You're the architect; build accordingly.

Use Reflective Language

People are drawn to people who sound like them. It's psychology, not sales.

If someone greets you with “Yo,” responding with “Good morning, esteemed customer” probably won’t cut it.

Mirror their energy. Match their tone. Adapt; don’t act. You’re showing them you’re on their wavelength, and that simple shift builds comfort fast. Meet them in their world, and they’ll invite you into their thinking.

Love the One You’re With

When you’re in a conversation, be in the conversation.

Not half-listening while checking emails. Not planning what you’ll say next. Just be present.

People can feel when you’re distracted, and nothing kills trust faster. So close the tabs, literal and mental, and give the person your full attention. They’ll notice, and they’ll appreciate it.

Give First, Receive Last

Demonstrate trust before expecting them to trust you.

Show respect before expecting it from them.

Demonstrate that you can listen before they will listen to you.

Demonstrate honesty and transparency before you expect it back.

Good relationships are built on trust, honesty, and mutual respect. You can’t expect someone to reciprocate these qualities unless you demonstrate them first.

Here’s an example of how you can do that in your first twelve words:

“Is this a bad time for you to take a recruitment call?”

In under eight seconds, you've managed to sound like a decent human being, a rare feat in this industry.

Why it works:

Saying "*bad time*" shows respect for their schedule.
Mentioning "*recruitment call*" demonstrates honesty.
Offering them an easy way out builds trust.

By starting with these principles, you're setting the tone for a genuine and respectful conversation.

Why Building Real Relationships Pays Off

- You're remembered long after the call ends, even if nothing comes of it today.
- You reduce ghosting, rejection, and resistance because the conversation feels human again.
- You differentiate yourself in an industry full of noise simply by being authentic.
- You stop chasing short-term wins and start building long-term gains.

If relationships are the foundation, then great questions are the tools that build them. Not just any questions; the kind that create a pause, spark insight, and show people you're paying real attention. The type that shifts conversations from small talk to substance.

Traditional questions next. Bring a proper Yorkshire brew.

Relationships Rap-up

The Real Deal

Yo, you can charm, you can chat, you can smile on cue,
But real connection? That cuts straight through.
Ain't in the pitch or the sweet talk tricks,
It's what you do when it's awkward as sh*t.
Forget the quick wins, bin rehearsed lines,
Come correct, with presence and signs.
This ain't about charm or fake interaction,
It's trust, it's care, it's a human connection.
Show up, stay real, don't lose your grit,
'Cause the ones who fake it just chat sh*t.
Respect in your tone, intention in your view.
That's how we roll...The **Clean Soul Crew**

Chapter 3
Traditional Questions
Truth or Tactic

Humans have been asking questions ever since we realised that merely pointing and grunting were not enough to get a biscuit.

As toddlers, we unleashed a relentless "*Why?*" at weary adults who eventually resorted to the classic response, "*Because I said so!*" Asking questions is instinctive. It helps us make sense of the world around us.

In recruitment, however, the questions we ask do much more than gather information. They have the potential to connect us with another person or completely derail the process. When used effectively, questions can foster trust and provide valuable insights. When they are not, they can lead to ghosting, confusion and misinformation.

But how often do we actually stop and listen, I mean really listen, to the questions we ask? And more importantly, how do they land?

Let us take a step outside ourselves for a moment.

An NDE Exercise

Yes, you are right. That does stand for Near-Death Experience. More commonly known as eavesdropping, but I love a bit of drama. You will need to sit among other recruiters for this, but do not tell them what you are up to. Simply scroll through LinkedIn or a job board, pretending to conduct research or look for candidates.

You are now going to hover above your colleagues' phone conversations. I know you cannot hear the person on the other end, so you will need to channel yourself into the shoes of that prospect, client or candidate. You will hear candidate screening conversations on most calls, as that is where we spend the majority of our time. Your mission is to take mental notes of how you would feel and react to the questions being asked.

By the way, if you suddenly feel like you are travelling down a tunnel with a bright light at the end, get help immediately.

Welcome Back from the Other Side

Well done. You made it back. No doubt with a growing awareness that our questions do not always land the way we think they do.

Let us check out those observations.

Same Questions, Different Day

Chances are, you heard a familiar playlist of recruiter classics spinning on repeat:

What is your current situation?
What salary are you looking for?
Why are you leaving your current job?
What are you looking for in your next role?
Where have you been interviewed? (Asking for a friend)

Do you use agencies?

Sound familiar?

How Were the Questions Framed?

If you paid attention to the tone of the calls, you might have noticed that it was not always the questions themselves but how they were delivered that felt off. Here are a few common culprits:

Drill Sergeant
Talk me through your experience.
Why did you leave that job?
Barking orders rather than opening up.

Tip: If you have to ask a direct question like this, preface it with, "Could you" or "Would you..."

Multi-Choice
Are you looking to work from home or be based on site?
You are fed the answer. Multi-choice questions are great for online quizzes and nothing else.

Double-Barrelled
How did the interview go, and would you accept it if they offered?
Overload. One question. One response at a time.

Leading
You are not going to let me down on this interview, right?
Yes, because someone is definitely going to reply, "*Letting people down is kind of my thing.*"

Pitch-Slapped
Yes, it is a thing. It is when a recruiter launches into a monologue about an amazing, exclusive role they are working on, minus the three reasons why someone would not touch it with a disinfected stick, before asking any meaningful questions.

We do the same with prospects. We launch into sales mode about how brilliant and unique we are, the only recruiters in the world capable of solving their hiring headaches, before we have even established what the headache is.

Were you pitch-slapped during your out-of-body experience?

How Did This Exercise Leave You Feeling?

As your imaginary candidate, client or prospect self, reflect on this:

Did you feel comfortable enough to share your true motivators?
Did you trust the recruiter enough to be honest about why you are really leaving your job, or would you have defaulted to the trusty "*career progression*"?
Did you feel like your answers were shaped by how the question was asked?
Did you feel curious, engaged or heard?
Or did you feel like just another item on their to-do list?

If your internal reaction was, "*Actually... that felt a bit transactional*," congratulations. You have just had a front-row seat to what many people experience when speaking to recruiters.

Why Do We Do This?

If we know these conversations do not work, why do we keep falling back on them?

I get it. We are time-short and permanently busy. Between hitting KPIs, chasing clients, arranging interviews, sourcing candidates, writing job ads and updating the CRM, it is no wonder we default to quick-fire questions.

We need information quickly so we can move forward.

The Process Trap

We view our questioning as a process. As long as we have ticked the box that reveals XYZ, we have done our job.

Assumptions: The Silent Saboteurs

Ah, assumptions. Every recruiter's sneaky little frenemy. We assume we know what a candidate wants, what is essential to a client. We believe that just because someone has worked in an industry for ten years, they will be perfect for a job.

But assumptions are just educated guesses with a fancy title, and they are riddled with bias.

The truth? That person on the other end of the phone is not a job description in human form. They are a living, breathing human with unique decision-making criteria, motivations, drivers and emotions. They do not fit neatly into pre-labelled categories, yet we unconsciously allow our own assumptions to cloud our judgement.

The False Economy of Tried and Trusted

We lean on our go-to questions because they feel safe and efficient, but when you zoom out, they cost us more:

More time backfilling roles that blow up at the final stage
More candidates ghosting because they never connected in the first place
More back-to-the-drawing-board moments that leave us muttering at our monitors

That is not efficient. It is not time-saving. It is firefighting dressed up as productivity.

We are Teaching the Market How to Lie to Us

How we ask questions does not just affect what people say. It influences how truthful they feel they can be with us.

When we rush through calls, ask shallow questions, lead people to answers and frame things in ways that feel judgemental, we train candidates and clients to play the game.

So they:

Tell us what we want to hear
Avoid the truth about their doubts or concerns
Withhold deal-breaking details until it is too late

And then we get:

Counteroffers
Last-minute dropouts
Clients who change their minds
Ghosting
Rewrites
A LinkedIn post about how nobody has the decency to tell us they are dropping out of the interview

Frustrating? Of course, but hardly surprising.

When we ask questions that prompt people to give us the "right" answer, and we build our recruitment process on flimsy transactional data, it is no wonder the whole thing topples over at the worst possible moment.

Luckily, there is a better way.

But before we go there, take a breath. The next chapter will change the way you think about questions entirely.

Better questions next. Bring a builders (doubled bagged)

Traditional Questions: Rap-Up

Tactics & Tricks

Yo, all the questions were dead on arrival.
Still wonderin' why there's no trust in the cycle?
"What's your salary?" "Why you leave?"
Drill sergeant bark, no time to breathe.

Multi-choice quiz with a built-in trap,
"Hours or your boss?", bro, it's all crap.
Double-barrel bullets straight through the soul,
"Would you take the job?" when you don't know the goal!

It's transactional, not relational,
Fast food questions, highly operational.
The old game's broken, time to transcend,
Real talk's coming... on the next bend.

Step quietly, next move's profound.
Less white noise. **The clean soul sound**

Chapter 4

A Different Question Altogether

Warning: This Might Ruin Basic Questions Forever.

In case you were thinking that I'm about to dust off the old traditional training manual that says all you need to do is ask open questions beginning with 'what', 'how', 'where', 'when', and 'why' then use closed questions when you want commitment or something decisive...

Nah.

Real conversations don't work like that. You seriously didn't think I was going to unpack and recycle that old shite, did you? No. You can take it straight back to the 1980s to retire in peace alongside shell suits, big hair, and *Top of the Pops*.

If assumptions, rushed calls, and standard questions aren't working...
If we want to move from shallow responses to genuine insight...
If we're going to stop interrogating and start collaborating...

Then it's time for something different.

Enter Depth Discovery Questions (DDQs).

The Swiss Army knife of recruitment conversations. These aren't your run-of-the-mill "tell me about yourself" lines. They are designed to cut through surface answers and get to what actually matters.

When you start using them, you'll notice you get to the truth faster, without the other person feeling cornered or handled.

What is a Depth Discovery Question?

From when I was knee-high to a gnat, my dad passed down two pearls of wisdom.

The first was: "*Zandy, you learn more by listening than you do by talking.*" As I was quite the chatterbox, this was probably his polite way of telling me to shut the 'F' up. Still, it stuck, far more than the usual "two ears, one mouth" line ever did.

The second? "*Never take anything at face value. Question everything.*"

Oddly enough, those two pieces of advice became the foundation for one of the most potent tools in recruitment: the Depth Discovery Question.

Most of the time, we're stuck taking responses from our market at face value because the questions we ask are built for data collection. We gather facts, timelines, job specifications, salary bands, reasons for leaving, the number of stakeholders, team size, and any other information needed to determine the best solution we can pitch back to them.

We collect ammunition.

When people sense their responses are heading towards a sales pitch, they start editing what they say. They recoil. They brace. The result? Rejection, ghosting, objections, or being fobbed off with vague answers. The door begins to close before we've even stepped through it.

DDQs change the dynamic into something far more interesting.

Instead of collecting surface-level answers, they explore thought processes: priorities, motivations, opinions, decision-making, and problem-solving strategies.

They don't just dig deeper; they hand over the shovel and invite the other person to start unearthing their own insights.

That's where the extraordinary happens.

Genuine understanding. Real revelations. Conversations that actually go somewhere useful.

By making self-discovery collaborative, these questions help you understand others better while allowing them to understand themselves. They create a pressure-free space where honesty flows, assumptions are set aside, and responses are direct.

If you're curious about what this looks like in real life, let's consider an example you'll likely be familiar with...

Delivering an Offer to a Candidate

Let's take a typical conversation. You've talked the candidate through the details: role, salary, benefits, working pattern, progression, and so on, gushing with enthusiasm and making statements like, "I've the best news ever for you."

The standard close might be:

"This is amazing, isn't it? Shall I go back to them to confirm your acceptance?"

Then, after three days of back and forth, the candidate backs out, or worse, goes radio silent.

Here's a DDQ that changes the entire dynamic:

"What parts of the offer would need to be revised for you to make a decision?"

That one question does several things.

It shifts their focus to their own decision-making criteria.
It opens the door to how they'll decide, not whether, but how.
It signals clearly that they can share unfiltered concerns.

It shows you what may need negotiating with the client.
It builds trust.
It gives them ownership of the decision.

It's the difference between guessing and knowing; reacting and anticipating.

How a DDQ Lands with the Listener

When someone is asked a Depth Discovery Question, it lands differently from most questions they're used to hearing.

Instead of responding automatically, there's usually a pause. it isn't because they don't know what to say, its because the question hasn't triggered a stock answer. It has sent them somewhere new.

They're no longer scanning for the safest response or the one that keeps things moving. They're checking in with how they actually see the situation, how they've been thinking about it, and what has been shaping their decisions up to this point.

As they sit with the question, something else often surfaces. They begin noticing the edges of their own thinking. More like small moments of recognition. The assumptions they've been carrying without testing them. The limitations or early warning signs they've never quite examined head-on, and sometimes didn't even realise were there.

They may think:

"Erm... that might be part of the problem."
"I've never actually thought about it like that."
"I'm not sure why we do it that way."

This is usually where the pause stretches a little longer, and it isn't anything to worry about. In fact, that's when you know it's working. (Always give them three seconds before speaking.) The brain is no longer retrieving an answer; it's trying to process something new. That kind of thinking takes longer. It doesn't come neatly packaged.

So you might hear:

"I'm not sure."
"I've never been asked that before."
"Let me think about that for a second."

That tells you they've moved from describing their situation to examining it.

Once that shift happens, something interesting follows. The brain doesn't like loose ends. When people become aware of a gap, a conflict, or a potential risk, they naturally begin trying to resolve it themselves.

Yes, they start answering their own challenges, looking for ways through, around, or out of them.

That's often the moment they begin asking their own questions. They're trying to work out what to do next. When your input is invited at that stage, it lands very differently.

It's no longer you advising from the outside. It's them seeking insight to support thinking that's already underway.

That's when it becomes a two-way conversation rather than an interrogative session.

How a DDQ Shifts Thinking

Before we go any further, I need to be crystal clear about one thing. This is not a lesson in how to construct the perfect Depth Discovery Question. You don't need a framework memorised, a laminated prompt card, or a philosophy degree tucked under your arm.

What is useful, though, is understanding why these questions land differently in the brain. Once you understand that, you'll stop trying to sound clever and start sounding curious. That's where they earn their keep.

Think of this as a peek under the bonnet.

These questions are not designed purely to extract information, although you will still get everything you need to know. Their real purpose is to take the listener further than they would normally go and unlock a piece of thinking that hasn't yet been examined.

Now, you might be tempted to think that's easy. I'll just ask things like:

"What motivates you?"
"What challenges are you facing?"
"What concerns do you have?"

Nice try.

Those questions still keep people firmly in surface-response mode. They know the answers they're expected to give, so they give them. Polite. Edited. Safe.

A DDQ works because of where it has to travel in the brain to retrieve what is real and true.

I'm a recruiter, not a neuroscientist, but here's the bit that matters.

The brain is constantly filtering information. If it didn't, we'd all be rocking in corners muttering about breakfast cereals. When a question lands, the brain instantly prioritises it and decides where to go to retrieve an answer.

Let's demonstrate something simple.

"What did you have for breakfast this morning?"

That's a straightforward retrieval task. The prefrontal cortex assesses it, the hippocampus retrieves the memory, and out it comes: tea and toast.

Minimal effort and engagement. Useful, but shallow.

Now let's try something more complex:

"What did you have for breakfast three Tuesdays ago?"

Suddenly, the brain has to work overtime.

Unless you eat the same breakfast every day, or never eat breakfast, retrieving this information becomes difficult. The brain starts rummaging through long-term memory, reconstructing days, routines, and events, and then usually draws a blank.

Now watch what happens with a DDQ.

"What sort of breakfast would you treat yourself to on a payday Friday?"

A different gear entirely.

This question doesn't ask the brain to retrieve information; it asks it to create meaning and context.

The prefrontal cortex kicks in for imagination and evaluation. Sensory memory gets involved. Emotion, preference, desire, and values all come into play. People picture it. They feel it.

That's the difference.

A standard question asks for facts; a DDQ activates thinking.

When a DDQ works well, it tends to do three things:

It connects to something real that they recognise.
It invites reflection rather than defence.
It gives their thinking somewhere to land.

You don't need to consciously build these elements into every question. In fact, trying to do so usually makes things worse, because you'll be too focused on how you sound rather than on the listener's experience.

What Needs to Be in Place for a DDQ to Work

Throughout my recruitment career, when people around me have gone into full NDE mode and said, "*Ooh, that's a good question to ask*," they make a note of it, and some even ask me to make them a list. Then they use them, verbatim, and it doesn't work.

There's a reason for that.

The words you use, although still very important, will not cut it unless the following is also in play.

Active Listening

This is key to the success of these questions and goes deeper than just hearing their responses.

Surround each DDQ with clarifying, summarising, and validating questions and statements to make sure you truly understand the context of the response. They are great for giving you little checkpoints and signals throughout the conversation. They also encourage the person to come back with more information, and demonstrate that you are listening. When your market feels heard, they are more likely to listen to you when it's your turn to speak.

Listen out for the pauses, the longer silences, and also for when one of your questions has hit a raw nerve.

It's not uncommon to come across this. People put their heads in the sand and don't want to confront what they need to. They may even be a little defensive, in a "*What have you asked me that for?*" or "*I don't even want to think about that*" sort of way. Don't force it or try dissecting it, because they will do that automatically anyway. Even when the conversation is over, it can set off a train of thought without you.

When listening to detailed information, lean in, either towards your phone, screen, or in person. It helps you keep track. Lean back if their response is more general and easy to follow.

Aside from listening to them, also self-monitor how you are sounding, self-NDE. How would you answer the question you have just asked them? Are you countering and trying to justify your reasoning in response to what they've said? It helps to keep yourself in check.

And as my dad used to say:

"You learn more by listening than you do by talking."

Mindset

If you ask Depth Discovery Questions without operating from a them-first mindset, people will sense it.

The problem isn't that the question fails to retrieve the "right" information. The reason it's likely to fall flat is what happens after they respond.

The moment they say something you don't agree with, it's easy to slip into persuasion mode. Before you know it, you're mentally building a counter-argument while nodding politely and pretending you're still listening.

Your follow-up questions start nudging and reframing, steering the conversation towards the answers you were hoping for all along.

That's when the listener senses you're operating from getting your own needs met. They recoil, filter what they say, and the guard comes back up.

A DDQ asked with an agenda stops being a DDQ.

Relationships

When people copy a Depth Discovery Question and it falls flat, it's easy to assume the wording was the missing piece. It wasn't.

What made the question land originally wasn't the phrasing. It was the human connection already in play when it was asked.

DDQs invite people to think out loud. For that to happen, the listener has to feel safe and protected from being judged, corrected, and being steered towards a particular response.

That level of safety doesn't come from rapport techniques or polished delivery. It comes from taking ownership of creating the relationship in that moment. The listener can spot the difference when the conversation is genuinely about understanding them.

When that safety is present, people relax and stop editing themselves. They give you answers that are far more useful.

It doesn't matter if the conversation is short-lived, with no next step or commercial gain; the questions still land well. People leave feeling heard rather than handled.

Without that relationship in place, even the most carefully phrased DDQ becomes just another question and, once again, the depth disappears.

Pulling It All Together

Recruiting with a Clean Soul is a methodology. A triage. A three-relational system where a them-first mindset, intentionally created relationships, and questions feed each other. Take one away, and the others collapse.

DDQs give you the tools that cut through the noise and reach something real. Use a DDQ without the other two? It's just a line in a script. Use all three together? That's when it shifts.

Questions without the right mindset turn manipulative.
Questions without a relationship turn superficial.
These two principles, without the right questions, never quite get off the ground.

That's what makes this a methodology and not just another training manual filled with techniques to memorise and forget.

In Parts Two and Three, you'll see plenty of real-life examples of DDQs in action across prospects, the job take-on, and candidates. You will notice how the conversations stop being transactional and start doing something useful.

How DDQs Will Benefit You

- No more reliance on playing the numbers game and just picking up the phone to get your KPIs in. Having high-quality calls means you will be happy to make them, and this will show up in your ratios and pipeline.
- You will be able to qualify or disqualify your calls without the sting of rejection.
- You will be able to pre-empt and help your market navigate potential obstacles long before they derail the recruitment process, saving you time on those "back to the drawing board" moments.
- You will have richer, deeper, more satisfying conversations, even if they don't lead to anything, making your pipeline more solid.
- You will only work on the most commercially viable vacancies.
- You will, get clearer commitment from candidates.
- You elevate your personal brand by building trust early in every conversation.
- You will unearth more opportunities to generate revenue that may otherwise be missed.

FAQs

Right, a few frequently asked questions, because this chapter is about asking questions and, no, the irony isn't lost on me.

Q: Will a DDQ hypnotise a prospect to want a retained assignment, fall to their knees in admiration, and ask how soon they can sign my terms?

A: Sadly, no. If they did, then this book would be shorter, cost four times as much, and I would be sunning myself on some exotic beach. What they will do is get you to the truth a lot faster.

Q: Are there any negatives to using DDQs?

A: Yes. Sometimes you ask one brilliant question and, before you know it, the floodgates open and you are getting chapter and verse on their gluten-free diet and their dog's separation anxiety. You might be tempted to rein them in with a "Sounds great, but let's get back on track." But this will quickly break trust.

Just suck it up and roll with the punches. It will eventually stop. Your ears have my deepest sympathy.

Q: Are there any questions I should avoid?

A: Yes, there are a few. The primary one is asking the "why" question, because it forces people to justify their decisions and can make them defensive. Also, avoid any questions, that lead them to the answers you want to hear.

Q: What if the person I'm talking to is a complete knob?

A: Then the red flags will present themselves very quickly. DDQs won't magically turn a knob into a delight or rehabilitate a full-blown twunt. What they will do is show you exactly who you're dealing with, early enough.

Q: When do we use DDQs?

A: We can use them in every recruitment conversation we have. However, this book focuses mainly on the qualifying stage, which is when we unwittingly inflict the most damage.

Q: Are DDQs just consultative questions with a new, quirky title?

A: No. Consultative questions help you work out what's going on. DDQs help them work it out, which is why they tend to land harder and stick longer.

Q: Do DDQs work over email or LinkedIn messages?

A: In my experience, no. I've tried it more than once, and it tends to come across as a bit gimmicky. That's because, in writing, people can't sense the mindset, and the intention to build a real relationship isn't there yet either. Without those two things in play, the question just reads like... a bunch of clever words.

Q: Do you ask DDQs in any sort of order?

A: Yes, we do. These questions take people on a journey. Ask them in the wrong order, you get noise. Ask them in the right order and you get movement.

I'm so glad you asked me that, because that's where Chapter 5 comes in.

Triple E Journey next. Bring a flask.

DDQ Rap-Up

Depth Charge

Yo, we binned the script, flipped the switch,
Old school lines? Nah, they don't hit.
Ain't here for "Where, Why and When,
Rinsed and repeated ten times ten.

DDQs, man, spark that flame,
Locked-in focus, not playin' no game.
They don't chase facts; they rewire thought,
Pullin' out answers they ain't been taught.

They think it's awks, we know it's not,
The pauses, that's where things unlock.
No rush to rescue, no need to save,
That space is the power recruiters crave.

We ain't in this to fake or sell,
We tune to the truth, and we do it well.
So next time you're ghosted, blanked or stalled,
Don't blame them, your Qs just called.

Drop it down good, load it right,
And flip that convo like Friday night.

Chapter 5

The Triple E Journey

A Trust-Building Masterclass and Objection Prevention Programme

Welcome to the dirty little secret of recruiting with a clean soul. The Triple E is the framework that brings the three principles together and takes our market on their buying journey. The beauty of it is that it massively reduces your need to pitch, sell, or persuade.

It guides candidates, clients, and prospects through three deceptively simple stages:
Exploration. Evaluation. Expectations. (We will be looking at these individually next.)

It's the heartbeat that runs throughout every conversation in this book, and once you understand it, you'll start to see the real reasons why deals collapse or come together seamlessly.

It's a No From Me

You've put in the graft, said all the right things, and kept everyone engaged, and then, as if out of nowhere, it goes pear-shaped.

A candidate goes cold, a client changes their mind. Someone suddenly "doesn't feel quite right" about moving forward, and there you are, staring at your inbox like it's going to apologise.

Our instinct is to influence it, talk them back around, reassure them, but by then, the horse is already halfway to Scotland. They've made their decision, and they'll either ghost you or offer a reason that sounds plausible but skirts the truth. This isn't dishonesty. They're just protecting themselves from being told they've made the wrong call. No one likes to be confronted with "you've made a bad decision".

So, ultimately, we brush it off. "*It happens.*" "*It's the nature of the beast.*" "*We're dealing with people.*"

Of course, not every process derails. Sometimes, with a good wind behind it, it all lines up. If it didn't, we wouldn't have an industry, but far too often, everything rests on a knife-edge, and no deal is truly safe until someone walks through the door and starts the job.

Whether it all goes ahead or crashes and burns depends on one thing only...

These aren't casual decisions either. They're not "*what shall I have for lunch*," they are disruptive, emotional, and high-stakes for everyone involved. They're made under pressure, shaped by invisible influences, internal politics, fears, and expectations that often go completely unspoken.

No matter how persuasive I was, how prepared I felt, or how carefully I managed the process, some of those decisions still slipped through my fingers, and when they did, they rarely gave a warning. Eventually, I had to accept that if I wanted to stop losing good outcomes to last-minute uncertainty, I had to change where I was placing my attention.

So, I changed my approach, and the Triple E journey was born.

The Back to Front Game Changer

The more I looked at what was going wrong, the clearer it became: I'd been focusing on the wrong part of the process.

So, I shifted my attention to the very first conversations I was having with my market; when I was qualifying a job with a hiring manager, trying to win new business from a prospect, or speaking to a candidate for the first time. (By the way, the word screen will have a suitable funeral in Chapter 9, flowers optional.)

I realised that if I could uncover the factors influencing their decision-making right from the start, I'd have far more confidence in predicting which opportunities would land and which were always going to collapse.

I started crafting depth discovery questions (see Chapter 4). These helped people visualise their future, confront potential roadblocks, and identify any red flags. I stripped out bias and assumptions, letting them respond in a way that felt safe and unpressured.

The information I gathered included:

Who else needs to be on board, and who's likely to throw a spanner in the works?
What's holding them back from achieving their goals?
What's missing from their process, their search, their thinking?
How would hiring someone affect the team dynamics?
How would changing jobs affect their home and life balance?
How will they know when a role, a candidate, or a recruiter feels right?

When I first started doing this, the shift was so immediate and dramatic that it stopped me in my tracks. It was as if I'd been walking around in the dark for years and someone had finally switched the light on. Suddenly, conversations that used to skim the surface went deep fast, and the ripple effect through the whole process was unmistakable.

Here's what changed:

Engagement like I'd Never Seen Before:

Their answers were thoughtful. Unfiltered. Honest. Even over the phone, you could hear them leaning in. What began as a simple exchange of information turned into a two-way flow of trust, something that had been missing in so many "qualification calls" before this. No more sounding like I was reading off the back of a Cornflakes box.

Self-Discovery and Ownership:

People started recognising their own blind spots, red flags, and obstacles, things they hadn't realised were even there, and once they identified them, they began finding solutions, which meant they were taking ownership of the path forward instead of being dragged along by me.

Openness to Advice:

Because the conversation felt safe and unpressured, they were more willing to ask for insights when they hit uncertainty. It stopped being a pitch and started feeling like a collaboration.

Early Understanding of the Right Fit:

By re-examining their goals with fresh eyes, they could decide early if an opportunity was worth pursuing. It saved wasted time, energy, and emotional investment on both sides, and spared me the joy of discovering halfway through an interview that their dream job was anything but this.

Radical Honesty when Walking Away:

If something didn't feel right at any stage, they told me, without disappearing. Even when they dropped out, the relationship stayed intact, not ghosted.

A Stronger, more Reliable Pipeline:

Last-minute "no" decisions at crunch time dropped dramatically. Although fewer people reached the final stage, those who did landed successfully. No more crossing my fingers and hoping a decision would go my way; my pipeline became solid and predictable.

The Ability to Spot the Wrong ones Early:

I could see much sooner if a candidate or client was going to be a nightmare. And like most recruiters, I've had those "never again" moments, the kind where, in hindsight, you wouldn't have touched them with a bargepole. Now, I could avoid them altogether.

They Revealed How they Buy:

Perhaps the most valuable outcome of all: my market began showing me exactly how they made their buying decisions. They told me what mattered most, who influenced them, the steps they took before committing, and what would stop them in their tracks. Once I understood this, I didn't have to guess how to sell to them; I could align my approach perfectly with how they wanted to buy. It was like being handed the cheat codes, without having to marry the Sims character to get them.

All of the above, the deeper engagement, honesty, stronger pipeline, spotting the wrong ones early, and knowing exactly how my market bought, wasn't luck; it was the direct result of asking the right questions, in the right way, at the right time.

In the next sections, we'll break down each stage of the "*Triple E*" in turn, so you can see how they work together to influence decisions from the very first conversation and carry that influence to a confident "*Next Steps*".

This is NOT a sales process. It's a replacement for those "Are you interested?" initial calls. This is different in that it qualifies or disqualifies with greater certainty, less rejection, and fewer things slipping through the cracks.

Done right, it stops feeling like a ball-aching numbers game and becomes a more enjoyable, enriching conversation. Whilst it may seem more protracted than your regular initial call, it will prove to be invaluable when a recruitment process gets underway.

This journey has three stages:
Exploration – Current situation
Evaluation – Baggage check
Expectations – Alignment and readiness to change

I will be using a train metaphor for this journey in order to make it easier to keep track (see what I did there?).

Please bear in mind this isn't your average commute. You may wish to observe the following crew conduct manifesto before departure.

CREW CONDUCT MANIFESTO

Welcome aboard, Recruiters.

Before we roll out, a quick reminder of our duty of care. We are responsible for every passenger who boards this train. They trust us to get them where they need to go, not where we'd prefer them to go.

- No persuading passengers to take a route they didn't ask for. Detours for commission are strictly off-track

- "Fantastic opportunity," "stand-out candidate," and other hard-sell announcements are cancelled until further notice. Keep the sales patter in the buffet car.

- Leading questions, manipulation, or destination-fixing will result in an immediate stop at Platform Ego.

- Collect information lightly, validate it carefully, and store it in empathy, not Excel.

- Remember: We facilitate their journey, and help them decide if this journey is the right one for them.

CHOO CHOO

Stage One Exploration

All Aboard

This stage is all about exploring their current situation. Hats off if we do it without actually asking, "*What's your current situation?*"

The exploration stage is broken down into three parts, which will cover where they are at the moment, how they got there, and their preferred or ideal situation. For the purpose of putting this into context for a journey, we are going to call them "*stops*".

There is no charge for this journey, and everyone is free to get off the train whenever they want.

The discipline here is brutal: no leading questions, no "*what's frustrating you most?*" bait, no fishing for the C-word (challenge). If they have any, they'll bring it up themselves.

Stop One: Today

Our job is to explore their internal world as it stands today. We start where they are now. Not where we think they are, not where we want them to be, but in their unfiltered present. This is the observation stage, where we ask without an agenda and give them the room to tell it like it is.

The best way to open them up is with a Depth Discovery Question, for example (to a passive candidate): "*How does your current role line up with what you hoped it would be when you joined?*" Obviously, adapt this to whoever you are speaking to.

This opens up the conversation and naturally leads to finding out how they are going about getting a new job, coping with a chaotic hiring process, or finding the relevant talent.

From here, we establish what seems to be working well for them, not what isn't.

If everything seems solid and they're where they want to be, then the conversation can stop there. Validate that success, let them know you're genuinely impressed. More often than not, they'll hesitate and reveal what's not working.

If they're truly content, just close with:
"If your situation changed and you found you needed some extra support, how would you go about selecting a recruiter you could trust?"

Stop Two: Yesterday

If your passenger's still on board, it's time to look at the events, circumstances, and triggers that brought them to this point. Chances are, when talking about their current situation, they've already thrown in a reason for leaving, feeling undervalued, or why the vacancy exists. Nothing wrong with that, but that's the surface-level, pre-polished version they hand out to recruiters.

Underneath? That's where you'll find the context, the good stuff: the real motivators and drivers, the fears they don't usually say out loud, and insight into how they make decisions.

When they tell the story in sequence, they don't just give you facts. They reveal turning points, half-baked fixes, decisions under pressure, and the forces that shaped their current outlook. This step is about finding the first shift that sets the wheels turning.

Now we have a clear idea of their current situation and how they arrived at that position. It's now time to look at the results or outcome that they ideally want.

Stop Three: Tomorrow

We already do a version of this when asking what sort of job they'd like, or what their ideal candidate looks like, but here, you're going further. What outcome or results do they want, and how important is that to them? This helps them to picture what "getting it right" would change in their world, what they value most, and what's at stake if it doesn't.

If you are still engaging with them, you may have been able to deduce if there is a gap between where they are now and where they would rather be.

Please, please, please don't be tempted to jump in with a solution just yet. We need to clarify and understand a great deal more about this before we drift into a monologue on how we can help them.

That's where we're heading now.

Next stage: Evaluation. Get your tickets and passes ready.

Exploration Rap-Up

All Aboard

Three stops in, taking in the view
Today's the chaos, yesterday's déjà vu.
Tomorrow's painted shiny and bright,
But don't grab a brush, it's not your fight.
They'll spill the truth when they're good and ready,
So keep that mouth shut and your ears steady.
No fixing, no flash, no "here's what I'd do,"
Just ride the rails, Clean Soul Crew.

Stage Two: Evaluation

Mind the Gap

If you find yourself at this point in the journey, there is a high chance you have sniffed out a need or a challenge that you can potentially help them solve. This is usually the point where we spring into action, armed with market insights, data, and good intentions, to position ourselves as the fix.

Do they listen to that and take it on board? Do they shorten their recruitment process because you have told them that they will lose candidates? Does the candidate not accept a counteroffer just because you have told them the data shows they will leave anyway within six months? Do they heck as like. It's a bit like being a parent giving advice no one asked for: well-meaning, nicely put, and totally ignored.

Our market is the same. Contrary to what you might think, they hate being educated, unless, of course, they ask for those insights. You are just a sender with no receiver; they're not listening.

If the train breaks down and we fail to get them to their destination, we blame them. The candidate was too picky, the HR manager dragged out the process for too long, and the Hiring Manager went with an internal candidate. Frustrating, isn't it, especially when we've already done all the work? The worst part? It's avoidable.

Let me explain:

Evaluation is all about digging deeper into the gap, the distance between where they are now and where they would rather be. Within the gap lies a whole load of baggage that consists of the following:

- Tangled systems, shifting priorities, and missing support.
- Personal doubts, hidden loyalties, and fear of change.
- Past scars, internal competition, and the pressure to deliver.

The main problem is that our passengers aren't really aware of them until they rear their ugly heads at the business end of the process, and if they don't see them, then neither do we.

This stage is about helping them unpack their baggage.

Our aim is to get them to look internally to see if they can pinpoint what is holding them back from reaching their endgame. The root cause of their problem might be as clear as day to us, but this is definitely, categorically a non-assumptive process, please read the crew conduct manifesto again. When they discover the root cause themselves, they naturally start thinking about ways to overcome it or prepare for it.

What we are Looking for:

Why they think they are not getting the results they want?
What seems to be missing from the way they are currently trying to get results?
What is standing in the way or preventing them from reaching their outcome?

This is where depth discovery questions come into their own, and in Part Two, you will see how to ask these with an unbiased perspective for each of the three elements of the recruitment dynamic.

When we go through this stage, a few things happen:

They see what could lie ahead rather than stumbling into it.
They see where old patterns might trip them up again.
They begin planning ways around the obstacles before they ap-

pear.
We both recognise if this journey is one we can take together.

Why It Matters

I'm not going to lie, this stage pushes everyone out of their comfort zone, but it also builds trust like nothing else, because once people recognise their obstacles, they stop resisting. They own the reality, and when they see it clearly, they're better prepared to deal with it, with or without you.

So now, the bags are lighter, the map's unfolded, and everyone knows where the toilets are. That's evaluation done right: honest, transparent, and a little bit braver than most recruiters dare to be.

Signals are green, track's clear, but before we pull away, we need to make sure every carriage is coupled tight.

That's what Expectations is all about, alignment before acceleration.

Evaluation Rap-Up

Track Side

Mind that gap, it's deep and rank,
Full of baggage that's never been frank.
Old habits leak with a dodgy smell,
But no one wants to look too well.
Excuses clatter, truth breaks through,
No sugar-coat, just what's true.
Tickets checked, tough talk due,
Stay on track with the **Clean Soul Crew.**

Stage Three: Expectations

Alignment and Readiness to Change

If Exploration was the **What.**
And Evaluation was the **Why.**
Then Expectations is the **How.**

For everyone to move forward and have a clearer idea of the direction they want to go in, we have to find out how ready they are to make changes.

Recruitment decisions only land cleanly when there is alignment. Everyone knows what "good" looks like and how they'll recognise it when they see it. Without that, people change their minds, misread signals, or chase the wrong thing.

Expectations are not about persuading them to come around to your way of thinking. It's about helping them define their own. You're guiding them to align the moving parts so, when a choice appears, a role, a candidate, or a recruiter, they'll know if it fits.

This stage is crucial in finding out how they would buy or buy into our services and also gives you a deep insight into how they make decisions.

What We're Really Finding Out in Expectations

- What needs to be aligned with their team, their business, or their family?
- What action would they need to take to ensure that everyone is on the same page?
- What service or process will they expect from us, a job,

or a candidate?

- How they'll recognise "right", what will make a candidate, job, or recruiter feel like the right fit?
- What is the impact or cost of not doing anything?
- What needs to happen next, the steps that turn a preferred outcome into a committed decision?

Why It Matters

Expectations close the loop on Exploration and Evaluation. This is not about winning the work; it's about helping someone see their path clearly. When people name what they want and how they'll know they've found it, they begin to take ownership. That's when hesitation turns into motion.
At this point, the next step isn't about persuasion, it's about direction. You're simply confirming how they want to move forward, at their pace and on their terms.
That's where one final question earns its place:
"What would you need to know about us, the job, or the candidate to feel confident that we could deliver on this?"
It gets them to explain how to sell your solution to them.
It bridges reflection with decision. If they're ready, it invites the conversation to continue. If they're not, it leaves them with understanding and respect intact. Either way, the train's still moving, and now they're choosing the track.
So now, if it's appropriate,
Go pitch that Fother Mucker.

Bringing It All Together: A Fluid Journey

The Triple E Journey looks like three distinct stages on paper, but in conversation it works more like a flow than a checklist.
One question in Exploration might open a door straight into Evaluation.
A response in Expectations might expose a blind spot you need

to loop back and explore.

A single Depth Discovery Question can glide someone through all three stages without them even realising it.

It isn't centred on rigid sequencing; it's more about following their thought process, keeping them in the lead, and using the stages as anchors rather than boundaries. The structure is there to guide you, not to box them in.

Expectations Rap-up

End of the Line

Final stop, Expectations station,
Where clarity meets collaboration.
No promises, no false impression,
Just lining it up with truth and intention.
Readiness to change, alignment gained,
Blind spots untangled, criteria reframed.
No push, no manipulation,
Just collaboratin' the expectations.
The Triple E guiding right through the mess,
Thanks for riding the **Clean Soul Express.**

Part One: Summary

By now, you'll have noticed what I was aiming for: to call time on the sell-it, fill-it, bill-it era. To show you how much of the "process" you were taught is nothing more than habit dressed up as gospel, and how fast it's becoming obsolete.

I wanted to push you out of your comfort zone, because that's the only way you start to see recruitment for what it could be: built on trust, not tricks.

I wanted you to hear the lie that "relationships" are just rapport and small talk, and see how they're actually the engine of everything.

Above all, I wanted to plant the idea that you can be the recruiter people talk about with respect.

My overriding intention in Part One was to give you hope. I wanted to remind you that this industry does not need to stay fractured; it can be turned around if we're brave enough to do the uncomfortable bit everyone else avoids.

Now that we have gone through the DNA of this methodology, the next part is where it gets real: clients, a job take-on, and candidates, live and unfiltered.

So, take a breath, pour yourself a strong one, and buckle up. The fun starts now.

Clean Soul Crew.

PART TWO

PART TWO
Principles in Action
Real Conversations

Principles in Action

We've covered the foundations, but nobody ever landed a client by quoting a principle. This is where we swap whiteboard wisdom for the messy, rubber-meets-the-road stuff that actually happens on the desk.

Now, cards on the table, I'm not a fan of "scripts". Too many sound like they've been written by someone who last spoke to a real prospect in 1998. Life's not neat. Conversations zig when you expect them to zag. People interrupt, swear, get distracted, or flat-out hang up.

So what you'll see in Part Two are not scripts to parrot back. They're real scenarios, stitched from lived experience, with all the quirks, pauses and eyebrow-raising moments left in. Alongside the dialogue, I'll break in with commentary to point out why something worked, or why it nearly went sideways. Think of it as subtitling the chaos.

We'll cover three fronts:

Clients: How to get past the brush-offs and "we don't use agencies" without sounding like a desperate double-glazing salesperson.

Job Intake: How to stop treating job descriptions like gospel and start uncovering the politics, blind spots and hidden landmines that really decide if a role gets filled.

Candidates: How to go deeper than "send me your CV" and get to who they are, what matters to them and if the timing is right.

By the end of Part Two, you'll have walked through the three elements of the recruitment dynamic separately and seen how Clean Soul principles change the outcome in each."

In Part Three, we'll pull it all together and show how those moving parts collide, and sometimes combust, when a process is under way.

You will see recruitment in its natural habitat: unpredictable, unfiltered and, if you lean in with the right mindset, surprisingly human.

Clients next. Bring a Red Bull.

Chapter 6
Clients

Rejection Hell: "The Prospecting Edition"

I recently read a LinkedIn post that was part inspiring, part eyebrow-raising, and wholly representative of our industry.

A renowned recruitment business development guru outlined a bold outreach strategy involving calls, emails, and DMs aimed at the same prospects twice weekly for three weeks. The claim? A 3% conversion rate. The result? A digital dust storm of comments from recruiters grappling with the concept of aggressive persistence versus professional pestering.

It's classic advice from someone who has had great success and still believes that this is what creates interest, but applying old-school methods to a market that has moved on is a mismatch.

We need a fresh perspective.

The numbers game has been played to death, and we're left cleaning up the debris of burned bridges, frosty prospects, and a reputation that's taken a hammering.

Years of being seen as pushy, persistent, and out of touch have left their mark, and not in a good way.

Moving away from this doesn't mean we do less; it means doing better.

It's about meaningful engagement over sheer volume and it works.

Rejection: It's Not Personal (WTF)

Welcome to one of the biggest lies we've ever been fed in recruitment. Rejection is personal. You know it, I know it, and the person trotting out the "*don't take it to heart*" line knows it too.

We're told it's part of the game. Take it on the chin, grow a pair, smile, dial, keep cracking on, and sooner or later you'll bump into someone desperate enough to need you.

The trouble is, after years of being brainwashed into believing it's not personal, we don't question how we're turning up. We ignore what our prospects are actually experiencing and keep playing the same rinse-and-repeat routine with a resilience label slapped on.

What we are actually doing is teaching our market how to reject us.

A quick reality check from LinkedIn

I was reminded recently just how quickly we personalise rejection in this industry.

A recruiter's post mentioned she started the day feeling motivated and upbeat, only to have that enthusiasm knocked sideways after a run of cold calls were shut down at reception. Phones put down. Conversations cut short. Frustration followed.

The conclusion? Receptionists were being rude. How very dare they. Why can't they just be nicer? They were damaging company brands. If they speak to recruiters like this, then how are they treating their customers? And "woe is me," recruiters once again being unfairly treated.

On the surface, it reads like a tale of rejection and disrespect. But underneath it sits something far more uncomfortable: a reminder of how often we personalise resistance rather than question the experience we're creating.

What stayed with me about this post wasn't the frustration; we've all had days like that. It was the decision to take the complaint to LinkedIn's rooftop in the hope that it would help change the behaviour of gatekeepers. Yeah, like that's going to make a difference!

Gatekeepers behave the way they do because, over time, we've taught them how to treat us. Repetition, familiar openings, predictable intent. We've become part of the background noise, and they are responding to a pattern we helped create.

There was also a subtle undercurrent of entitlement: the assumption that recruiters deserve a different kind of treatment simply by virtue of doing our job. That if only receptionists were nicer or more human, the problem would solve itself.

Receptionists don't exist to be warm and accommodating. They are literally paid to filter out sales calls. As a side note, gatekeepers can tell the difference between a sales/recruiter call and a customer simply by the way we breathe.

As for their rudeness damaging the company's reputation, I don't think any CEO in the history of commerce has ever said, "Our market share has dropped, it must be down to the way Emma on reception treats recruiters."

What matters here isn't whether rejection stings; it does. It's whether we're willing to take responsibility for the conditions that produce it.

If we keep showing up in the same way, using the same methods and making the same assumptions, we'll keep triggering the same response, just faster and with less patience each time.

Rejection isn't fixed by resilience; it's fixed by accountability.

Until we're prepared to change how we approach the market, all the LinkedIn venting in the world won't open a single gate.

The Traditional Recruitment Sales Process:

A Comedy of Errors

Before we dive into how the Clean Soul approach actually works on the desk, let's take a moment to salute the traditional sales structure, the noble, dusty path we've all stumbled down at some point.

It usually looks something like this:

Research and set call objectives
This is where we lose half a day on a company website that says everything and nothing, then deep-dive LinkedIn like amateur detectives, DM half their staff with a limp "*Hope you're well!*" and convince ourselves this is all strategic preparation.
Then we heroically set an objective: get on their PSL and maybe, if the stars align, nab a few urgent vacancies.

Introduction and generating interest
Ah, yes, the elevator pitch. Thirty seconds to sound compelling while they wonder if there's a polite way to mute you. In theory, magical. In practice, it's like lobbing spaghetti at a wall.

Ask probing questions to establish a need
Featuring the greatest hits: "*How many vacancies do you have?*" "*When does your PSL renew?*"
These aren't conversations; they're thinly disguised treasure hunts for pain points.

Explain how you can add value
Also known as, "*Let me tell you about all the features you didn't ask for.*"

Discuss pricing
Cue the awkward silence after you say the number and they try not to choke.

Overcome objections
"*We're happy with our current supplier.*" Translation: "*Why are you still talking?*"

Close and agree next steps
You suggest a next step and they say, "*Let me get back to you,*" and you spend the next week refreshing your CRM like it owes you money.

Wouldn't life be a whole lot better if BD didn't feel like medieval torture?

The Three Core Principles in Action

I'm not a big fan of scripts. They can be rigid, robotic, and completely miss the point of a genuine human conversation. However, I'm including the following three conversations to illustrate how the principles we discussed in Part One come to life when speaking with real people in real situations.

As you read through them, pay attention to a few things.

Mindset
We're not coming in hot with assumptions, pressure, or expectations. It's a non-transactional and clean-slate approach. No egos. No personal agendas.

Trust Building
The main objective throughout the calls isn't to close a deal or get a job on. The goal is to foster a safe environment for open and honest dialogue.

Questions
We're not steering the conversation toward a pre-planned outcome. We're helping them discover their own answers, regardless of whether it leads to anything now, later, or not at all. Notice how every response is followed by validation. This ensures they know we've heard them and allows us to pivot into the next question or explore further. Notice how they open up more when asked a

DDQ.

No Rejection
The first two conversations are cold calls, but with a notable difference. There's no immediate need and no burning problem to solve. Yet when those calls end, we don't walk away feeling rejected or deflated. We walk away with our integrity intact and our reputation upgraded.

Triple E Journey
The final call is a warm lead, the kind of conversation where there is a need. It's where we walk you through the Triple E from start to finish, showing you what it means to collaborate with integrity, curiosity, and depth.

So please don't treat these as templates; treat them as a window. A glimpse into what it looks like when the three principles of Recruiting with a Clean Soul come together in practice.

Questions to Avoid

Before we dive into the calls, let's pause to consider the types of questions recruiters typically begin with. You'll recognise them, the stock lines that sound logical but seldom build trust or provide the right information. In practice, they push prospects onto the defensive or shut the conversation down before it begins.

Here are a few of the most common, and how we can reframe them into questions that open doors.

AVOID: Are you recruiting right now?
REPLACE: What recruitment strategy has worked best for you when you've needed to hire?

AVOID: When's your PSL up for renewal?
REPLACE: How would you notice if your current PSL is no longer giving you the level of support you need?

AVOID: How is your current job advert for [vacancy] working out?

REPLACE: How has your recent hiring campaign for [vacancy] shaped your view of the candidate market?

AVOID: What are your current hiring needs?
REPLACE: How would a gap in your team impact your goals for this quarter?

AVOID: What are you looking for in a recruiter?
REPLACE: How will you determine if an external partner is capable of meeting your long-term hiring goals?

AVOID: What sort of challenges are you facing with hiring?
REPLACE: What's changed recently in the business that's made recruitment seem different?

A Final Thought Before we get Practical

Business development doesn't have to be a soul-sapping endurance test, and it certainly shouldn't require you to gird your loins before picking up the phone. If every outreach feels like bracing for impact, that's not resilience; that's your nervous system telling you something's off.

Now imagine this instead

How much business development would you actually do if rejection wasn't slowly eating away at your confidence? If it didn't linger in your chest for the rest of the day, colouring every call that followed? If "*no*" didn't feel like a personal failure, but simply information?

Imagine approaching conversations without trying to push, persuade, or perform. Without the subtle manipulation that comes from needing a result. Just curiosity, relevance, and a genuine sense of "*let's see if this makes sense.*"

When you stop trying to sell to everyone and start looking for the people who are likely to buy from you, your energy changes, your tone changes and, oddly enough, so do the outcomes.

Business development becomes lighter, more focused, and more human.

Your job starts to feel less like survival and more like something you're actually proud to do.

With that in mind, let's look at what this sounds like in practice...

Scenario One

Freezing Cold

This is an unsolicited prospect call. There's no particular reason to think they have any recruitment needs; in fact, there's every chance they don't.

I know there's a strong school of thought that cold calls are a relic of the past and, being frank, most people are more likely to screen an unknown number than answer it. It's understandable, but because hardly anyone does it anymore, those who do, and do it well, actually stand out.

In my experience, some of my best business relationships have started from calls like these. Not always immediately; sometimes it's a slow burn. But in a world full of "connect and pitch" LinkedIn messages, a real conversation, with no hidden agenda, still cuts through.

Me: Have I caught you at a bad time to take a recruitment call?

Commentary:
Always start with permission. It lowers resistance, respects their world, and signals that this won't be a typical sales ambush.

Prospect: It's never a good time, but we're just a small family business, so we wouldn't have any recruitment needs.

Commentary:
This could well be a brush-off. Instead of trying to overcome it, I'm going to ask a DDQ and listen out for any triggers.

Me: That makes sense. How do you keep the knowledge and skills in the business when the next generation has other plans?

Commentary:
This question does a lot of heavy lifting. It moves the conversation away from "need" and towards continuity, risk, and the future.

Prospect: Well, we seem to be getting by okay. The problem is we are running out of family. The younger generation just wants to be TikTok influencers.

Me: [Laughs] Yes, I've heard that one before. Is the whole business still family-run?

Commentary:
Humour breaks the tension, then the follow-up expands the context.

Prospect: There are six family members and 27 employees in total. Mind you, the majority of us are either past retirement age or approaching it soon, and this generation doesn't seem interested, unfortunately.

Me: Have you ever had to recruit anyone from outside your circle before?

Prospect: We are pretty niche, so we know everyone in the industry who lives locally. We've never really gone all out to recruit anyone. People seem to want to work here; we pay well, have a good reputation, and we are always busy.

Commentary:
See how he is now starting to talk? It's clear he is locked in a complacency bubble. If it ain't broke...

Me: It sounds like you've built something solid. What do you imagine it's like finding people with those same skills now?

Commentary:
Validation first, then a pivot into market reality. Notice: this question doesn't ask "is it hard?" It simply asks "what's it like?" That's a thinking question.

Prospect: With the rise of automation, it's a dying craft.

Me: That seems to echo what many of my engineering customers are saying. How are you planning to maintain your success in the future?

Commentary:
This is where future exploration begins: scenario thinking without pressure. I'm guiding him to widen the frame.

Prospect: We've never had a problem with work, so I've no plans to close the doors anytime soon. But I guess we need to put a succession plan in place.

Me: What would that look like?

Prospect: We considered taking on trainees or apprentices a couple of years back, but the consensus was that we would have to invest loads of time in training them, only for them to take that knowledge and leave.

Commentary:
Reflect the concept back to him. Don't define it; let them build it.

Me: Yes, that's a fair concern. What else do you think might help maintain the business's continuity?

Commentary:
This question digs deeper into the belief system behind the obstacle.

Prospect: We're already bringing in more automation and technology to keep pace, so we're less reliant on the existing skill set.

Me: That's a smart move. How well do you think your current team will adapt to that shift?

Commentary:
This takes them into the ripple effects: stakeholders, impact, and internal capability. Crucial territory.

Prospect: Well, they are all a bit long in the tooth now and don't want to change their ways, so we might have to start thinking about exploring what's out there.

Me: Would you be able to tap into your existing network for this?

Commentary:
This question hands the reins back to him. He now defines his own trigger point, which is far more potent than me giving him one.

Prospect: Most are old school. We might have to look outside, though we wouldn't be doing anything for at least 12 months.

Me: I totally understand; you seem to be managing just fine as you are. How would you know it was the right time to get some external help with your future plans?

Prospect: Well, if my own workers were not coping well with automation, it could affect our customers. Maybe I need to get the ball rolling sooner rather than later. Would you be able to send me over your details, and perhaps we can pencil in a meeting in the new year?

Me: I certainly can. I would love to see the operation and assess whether I could be the best person to help with this.

Prospect: Oh, thanks, that would be great. Let me give you my details...

What Made This Conversation Different?

No bloodhound behaviour. We didn't sniff around looking for a hint of hiring pain to pounce on.

Instead, we asked permission before every move. We respected that they're already doing a great job. We made no assumptions that they needed me. We surfaced potential future changes without suggesting they have a problem now.

The focus was on their thinking: on them evaluating where they want to be and what might stand in the way of that. Not me pushing, but giving them the space to realise, or not realise, future needs on their terms.

The Result

We went from "I never need to recruit" to "please send me your details." That's the difference between outright rejection and future potential.

I may not get anything out of this in the short term, but I've now laid the groundwork to follow up and see where it leads.

Scenario Two:

Actively Recruiting

Rather than an unsolicited prospect call, I noticed that this company had been advertising for a Technical Estimator. The advert had been live for over a month and specifically stated, "No agencies." Normally, that would send recruiters sprinting for the hills or pitching harder, but this is about showing up respectfully, opening up their thinking and, if appropriate, offering support.

Prospect: Hi, Sharon speaking.

Me: Hi Sharon, have I caught you at a bad time to take a recruitment call?

Sharon: It's never a great time, but I've got a few minutes. We do all our recruiting ourselves, though. What's this about?

Commentary:
The boundary appears early. No *need to challenge it, just acknowledge it and work with the world as it is.* Notice *how I have not introduced myself? She doesn't care who I am. She isn't listening to me yet.*

Me: I appreciate that, and I'm not looking to disrupt what you're already doing. I noticed you've been advertising for a Technical Estimator for a while. How did this particular search shape your view of the candidate market?

Commentary:
Validation first, then a curious, non-threatening question. Not "Do you need help?" but "How has this been for you?" That distinction keeps the door open.

Sharon: It's been hard work, honestly. But we've just made an offer, so I think we're sorted now.

Me: That's brilliant news, congratulations. When you think back over the process you used, what stands out the most?

Commentary:
One clean question. No fishing for pain. Just an invitation to reflect, which naturally brings the truth to the surface.

Sharon: Well, the job postings didn't bring in anyone decent. In the end, we approached someone we knew from a competitor, and that's who we offered the job to.

Me: Sounds like you had to put quite a bit of effort into getting someone right. What helped you decide to switch from relying on the advert to going direct?

Commentary:
This explores the pivot point, the exact moment their internal process reached its limit. This is called the trigger.

Sharon: We just weren't getting anywhere. We don't usually struggle, so it took us by surprise. Going direct felt like the only option left.

Me: That makes sense. When you're reviewing applicants from the adverts, what's your usual process?

Commentary:
Now we're mapping their internal system to gain understanding, not to prepare her for a sales pitch. This is where blind spots surface organically.

Sharon: I sift them myself, shortlist a couple, and if they look promising, we bring them in. But this time, nothing really matched.

Me: It is still a very tough market for skilled candidates. It sounds like you've got a very hands-on process. When things slow down, as they did here, how do you usually decide whether to broaden your approach?

Commentary:
You're not asking "Why don't you use agencies?" You're asking how she makes decisions. Much safer. Much deeper.

Sharon: We only widen it if we have no choice. We prefer not to use agencies; it gets messy. We've had mixed experiences in the past.

Me: I see. What experiences have influenced the way you prefer to handle things in-house?

Commentary:
This is the moment the "no agencies" rule gets explored gently and indirectly, without confrontation. She'll reveal more than she would if you asked directly.

Sharon: Mostly pressure. Agencies rush us, push candidates, and ignore what we tell them we want. And once you say yes to one, they all pile in.

Me: I can appreciate why you'd want to protect your process. When your adverts weren't producing the right people, what helped you decide it was time to change tack?

Commentary:
Notice the theme: every question is designed to help her inspect her internal systems. Her world. We are not asking questions to justify our reason for calling.

Sharon: Honestly? We were stuck. We'd exhausted the adverts, increased the budget and still got nothing. That's when we approached the guy directly.

Me: Your flexibility probably made the difference there. If something unexpected happened, say the candidate changed his mind during his notice period, how prepared would you feel to start again?

Commentary:
This is the future risk question. Not fearmongering, just surfacing reality so she joins the dots herself.

Sharon: Oh God, don't say that. We'd be back at square one, I guess, and we don't have anyone else in the pipeline. At that point, we'd probably look at agencies, but I wouldn't even know where to start.

Me: Of course. Given the challenges this time, what would a trustworthy agency need to show you to make you feel comfortable involving them?

Commentary:
This is the buying-criteria question. They tell you exactly what they would need from you, in their own words.

Sharon: Someone honest, no pressure. Someone who listens and actually understands what we need, and not just chuck us CVs over.

Me: That makes perfect sense. Would it help if I sent over a brief overview of how I work, so you've got something on hand if you ever want to explore support in the future?

Sharon: Yes, that would be useful. Send it over and give me a call at the start of next month. By then, I'll know if everything's gone smoothly with the new guy.

Why this Conversation Worked

Very early in this call, we knew there was zero chance of walking away with a job to fill. Sharon had already found her man, signed him up and was practically halfway through planning his onboarding. The goal here was never to swoop in like a recruitment hero. It was simply to understand how her hiring world works without triggering her "No Agencies Allowed" forcefield.

Instead of pretending we've got a drawer full of Technical Estimators on standby, we stayed curious. We explored her process, her pain points and the mysterious inner workings of her no-agencies rule.

By letting her talk through what actually happened, the panic, the advert graveyard, the budget stretch and the eventual "sod it, let's just headhunt someone ourselves" moment, she ended up mapping her whole system for us without even realising it.

Because we didn't challenge her stance or tell her how ineffective her process was, she felt safe enough to admit what wasn't working, what nearly broke and what she'd need if things ever wobbled again.

She told us the qualities she'd need from an agency she would trust.

She laid out the criteria.

She opened the door.

She did it without us having to push or persuade, because she didn't feel sold to.

So no, this wasn't a job on. This was a small masterclass in turning a "No agencies, thanks" into "Send me your details and call me next month." No pitch-slaps or pressure. Just a clean, human conversation that positioned us as the future Plan B, the one she defined herself, for the day her shiny new hire gets cold feet and decides to go backpacking around Bali.

And that, dear recruiter, is how you make an impression without making a scene.

Scenario Three:

Warm Lead

In this case, I already have a warm introduction.

Tony, an Operations Director I've kept in touch with over the years, mentioned that Amber, their HR Manager, was struggling to find skilled candidates.

I originally met Tony as a candidate on a retained assignment several years ago. He didn't land the role, but we've kept in touch, shared each other's posts, and so on. I've never done recruitment for his current company, Nordalyn, so this conversation could potentially lead to new business.

This isn't a cold call; it's a warm one, with a shared history. Amber knows who I am but doesn't know if I can help. Our goal is to facilitate a conversation that lets her surface her own needs, challenges, and priorities so that by the time we discuss next steps, the solution feels natural, not forced.

You'll see a lot of commentary along the way, not because I like hearing myself talk (I promise!), but because I want to highlight the thinking behind each question, each reflection, and each decision to stay curious rather than get clever.

Let's dive in. Satnavs are optional. Curiosity is not.

We have already done the introduction, and Amber is happy for me to ask her some questions.

Exploration Stage

Me: I understand from Tony that you may be having difficulty attracting skilled staff. What's driving this recruitment need at the moment?

Amber: We've developed a product for the food processing industry. This is uncharted territory for us, which means we need individuals with specific skills to move it forward. I didn't think it would be so hard to find the skills we are looking for.

Me: Wow, it's rare to hear of this type of expansion in this climate. What kind of roles are you finding challenging?

Amber: These are mainly technical roles. We are looking to build a team of four or five over the next few months, and we cannot launch until we have the right people in place. We're way behind schedule.

Commentary:
Well, isn't that the equivalent of a recruiter's wet dream? They've just handed you the golden ticket to the recruitment chocolate factory. There is a definite need here: volume roles, a deadline to meet, and, obviously, not having much luck finding candidates.
So, what's your plan of action now? Let them know you have a secret stash of these people in your cloning laboratory out back? Drill down on the job specifics? Or explore a little more?
I don't know about you, but I'm starting to think this is too 'Christmas-has-come-early' for my liking. I don't know enough to hit her with a pitch, so I will continue exploring.

Me: That must be quite a stressful situation. How are you currently sourcing people with the right skills?

Amber: Generally, I post ads on LinkedIn and Indeed, and update our careers page.

Me: I see. What else have you got in place to help with this ambitious recruitment campaign?

Amber: What do you mean? It's just me doing it all. I've always done it this way; it's never been a problem.

Me: Crikey, I can't believe you are doing this all yourself. When you say you have always done it this way, what sort of prominence has recruitment taken before this product launch?

Commentary:
I am now exploring how she has previously recruited. It's clear she is biting off more than she can chew here, but I need her to recognise this.

Amber: It's always been manageable. No big recruitment campaigns, just replacing the odd person. We have excellent staff retention, so it's usually been okay. But I think I'm out of my depth here, as I don't understand the technical side of the roles.

Me: Some of the technical terms can be confusing. You mentioned that your main option for filling these roles was advertising them. What has the response been like?

Amber: Crikey, we've had loads of responses, but most have ended up in the no pile.

Me: Yes, job postings are like a box of chocolates; you never know what you're going to get. How has this shaped your view of the candidate market?

Amber: Oh, they're a fecking shower of sh*t. I mean, doesn't anyone want a job anymore? What's wrong with people these days?

Commentary:
If they start using colourful language, congratulations! You've reached a level of trust that only happens after a few too many pints at the pub. They're comfy with you, so enjoy the moment and reflect a toned-down version back to them, so they know they are safe to say it like it is.
A *different kettle of fish, though, if they are swearing at you!*

Me: You are right, it is sh*t. I struggle to understand them, but as a recruiter, I see fierce competition for skilled candidates. How are you presenting yourselves as an employer of choice to attract the right people?

Commentary:
This is a key question because it prompts Amber to consider how the candidate market impacts her hiring process. If she hasn't realised it, this moment will help her see potential gaps in how her company positions itself to candidates. In other words, if your 'chocolate box' is primarily full of nutty candidates who just don't fit, it might be time to re-evaluate your selection process or, more importantly, your employer brand. This question allows her to realise that without feeling like she's being "educated."
The goal is for her to reflect on her company's reputation from a candidate's point of view and recognise if she needs to make any changes to stay competitive.

Amber: I haven't given it much thought, but if there is a lot of competition for skilled people, I need to take a closer look at it. Come to think of it, we have had candidates recently who have turned us down because the salary was less than they wanted.

Commentary:
At last, the penny has dropped. It's as if she's just realised the hairdryer has been unplugged all along. Suddenly, everything falls into place, and the lightbulb moment is glorious. I now want her to start thinking about her future vision for how she intends to recruit, which may or may not include my services. I just have to trust the process.

Me: That must have been very frustrating for you. What do you see as being a more impactful recruitment process?

Amber: Good question. I believe it's crucial to have access to improved search resources beyond just job applications, and to invest more effort in ensuring a positive candidate experience. We should also review the packages we are offering.

Me: That sounds like a great way forward for you. How confident are you in doing that yourself?

Amber: I would love to think I could, but time is not on my side. I have been considering seeking help from agencies for a few weeks now.

Commentary:
At this point, it's tempting to whip out the cape, declare yourself "Agency of the Year," and ride in to save the day. But pitching now would be the recruitment equivalent of proposing marriage on the first date. Amber needs help, but we're not here to stick a plaster on a broken leg. We're here to understand the whole picture before offering a solution.

Let's Look at What's Come Out so Far:

- Volume Need: They need a team built quickly and can't launch without it.
- Resource Gap: Amber's flying solo, with no support or strategic hiring plan.
- Market Misjudgment: They underestimated the difficulty of the candidate market.
- Candidate Experience Neglect: No clear employer branding or competitive offer strategy.
- Sourcing Issues: Reliance on job boards with little success and mounting frustration.
- Self-diagnosis = ownership, which is key if we guide her through the following stages without resistance.

If we had jumped in too early, we might have had 4 or 5 jobs emailed to us, but we would have been recruiting on a shaky foundation, only to watch the whole thing wobble and collapse when unseen issues arose later.

So, before popping the champagne, we need to investigate the hidden obstacles and potholes that could derail this recruitment drive.

Evaluation Stage: Uncovering Obstacles and Blind Spots

Me: Thanks so much for being so open with me, Amber. It sounds like you've been doing an incredible job with what you've got; frankly, I'm impressed. What do you think has stopped you from going down the agency route until now?

Amber: The main barrier has been cost. We need to keep costs low, especially as we scale. I know the CFO will have kittens if we have to use agencies. What are your rates like?

Commentary:
This is a classic 'fear of change' obstacle. Amber has been used to dealing with her own recruitment and knows it isn't working for her, so she may feel inadequate.
And there it is, the inevitable "What's your rate?" moment; always about three conversations too early. If I try to answer this question, we will get into a negotiation wrangle, and I still don't have enough information to give her an accurate number yet. I don't even know the roles, and she doesn't have much of a clue either, so I will need to deflect this question.

Me: I can understand how important it is to keep costs low, especially as you scale. There are many variables to consider, such as the scarcity of candidates, the type of roles and the resources we'd need to calculate at this time. Once we know that, we can discuss various options that suit you. How would you address the costs of using an agency with the CFO?

Amber: I'd need to demonstrate that the value outweighs the cost. We'd need a detailed breakdown and justification of your fees, rebates and other expenses, and then compare this to the cost of any delays caused by not using an agency, particularly in terms of finding the right talent more quickly.

Me: Of course. What criteria will the finance team use to select an agency?

Amber: I will select, but they expect me to choose the cheapest option to keep our costs as low as possible.

Me: I understand. How would you assess whether the cheapest agency could deliver what you need in your urgent timeframes?

Commentary:
We've got a little dance going on, but if we don't nip it in the bud now, it will only crop up later. There is a high chance she will contact other agencies and spark a price war, which will eat into the time she doesn't have. I don't want to slam in a cheap rate right now, so I need her to consider service, speed and quality.

Amber: Erm, that's a good point. Finding the time to go through and weigh everything will be challenging. Getting the right people in who fit our culture is the main thing, so I have to consider the service and how quickly they can move. Price isn't the only thing I would consider.

Me: I know not all agencies are created equal. It sounds like a bidding war is the last thing you need on your plate right now. What would be the long-term impact on the company if you could not get agency support signed off?

Commentary:
Now she's thinking about how important it is to consider quality, service and time management, so she can better justify this to the finance team. I have now pivoted the conversation to examine the consequences of not taking any action.

Amber: (Pausing) We are already seeing this with delayed projects and the extra pressure we're putting on our staff. All the other countries rolling out this product are already operational, and we risk becoming a laughing stock. The head office is already asking us lots of awkward questions.

Me: Oh dear, I can imagine how difficult that must be. Who else needs to be considered when hiring for these roles?

Amber: Darren is heading up the new division. He reviews all the candidates, conducts interviews and decides who he wants on his team.

Me: I see. What push-back is he likely to have about being flexible on salary expectations and how the job is packaged to candidates?

Amber: He's a bit old-school and thinks everyone should be eternally grateful to come and work here.

Me: Oh, there's one in every company. How would you align his views with your vision of a better recruitment outcome?

Amber: I'll just have to tell him how it is, but you would probably be better placed to do that.

Commentary:
No love lost there, then.

Me: Okay, I can see that winning over Darren is key. You also face the challenge of balancing the budget with the need for quality candidates, and if the roles remain unfilled, it'll put extra pressure on the business. Ultimately, you need a hiring process that supports growth without compromising quality. Have I missed anything?

Amber: Yes, that's about right. Oh, and speed. We are running out of time. Tony laid it on thick about how thorough you were as a recruiter, and I can see where he is coming from. Do you think you could help us with this?

Commentary:
Ah, she's closing me. It's always lovely to hear that, but we've still got to ensure we're all building the same jigsaw puzzle, singing from the same song sheet or being on the same page, whichever cliché you prefer.

Before I race ahead and assume we're fully aligned, this is the moment to slow the pace, breathe and make sure we haven't missed anything lurking under the surface.

Expectations are where everything tightens up. It's where we check that what she believes she needs, what the business actually needs and what I can realistically deliver aren't three completely different stories pretending to be friends.

This stage also protects us both from the classic recruitment face-plants: mismatched timelines, invisible stakeholders suddenly standing up in the back row, assumptions about candidate quality and all the silent "I thought you were doing that" moments that can derail a brilliant start.

So, before we move forward, we're going to bring all the threads together and look at what she truly needs from a partner, not just what she thinks she wants today.

Expectations: Aligning What they Need

Me: Yes, I would like to think that I could. What support would you need from me to help you convince Darren and the CFO that using us would be the right direction for you?

Amber: That's a good question. Let's see. We'd need a transparent breakdown of your charges, rebates and other relevant details, as well as a solid understanding of how you would attract the types of people we need. It would be a great help if you could let us know how you have managed similar projects, especially if they are in the food industry.

Me: Got it. You need a breakdown of our business terms, which I can calculate once we have a better understanding of the roles. You also want to know what strategy we would implement to attract the best candidates, as well as examples of how we have successfully worked on similar projects. That's no problem. Apart from getting you the best candidates on the market, what else would you need to support the process?

Amber: Well, getting us the best candidates is the priority, but now that you mention it, perhaps things like salary benchmarking would also be helpful. And some advice on how we're presenting the roles, because if the salary is wrong or the messaging is off, it's no wonder we're struggling. Perhaps I should discuss this with the marketing team?

Commentary:
When the client adds extras to the shopping list without prompting, you're no longer pitching; they're convincing themselves.

Me: It sounds like you're already thinking quite strategically about this. What would be the best way for me to understand what you want to achieve as a company?

Amber: I suppose providing you with a better overview of our expansion plans and new products would help. It's not just about filling seats; it's about building a team to grow this division.

Commentary:
And there it is; the shift from 'fill my jobs' to 'help build my future'. Now we're getting somewhere.

Me: I get it. You are looking for a partner who can see the bigger picture, beyond firing CVs over.

Amber: Exactly. It needs to feel like we're working with someone who's an extension of our team, not just another supplier.

Me: That's precisely the way I love to work. Is there anything specific that would make you feel this collaboration was successful?

Commentary:
Notice how it's become a "we". We are heading into this together. It is starting to feel like a partnership, a collaboration, no push, no pull.

Amber: Ensuring the process runs smoothly from candidate search to offer, with regular updates and transparency. And, if you had any concerns about a candidate, you'd let us know immediately.

Me: Before we map out a plan, if we could address all the challenges you mentioned, what would this look like six months from now?

Amber: We would have a whole team up and running, and I could start tackling some of the HR initiatives I've had to put off and hopefully book myself a holiday.

Commentary:
We have gone through all the stages and must agree on how to proceed. At this point, I resist the urge to break into a little happy dance. She's selling herself on the idea, not me.

Next Steps: Building to a Close

Me: A well-deserved one, too. I believe that we can help streamline your hiring process and tackle some of your challenges. I worked on a similar project recently and can share the strategy I used. Would you be open to a follow-up discussion where I can present a tailored approach that fits your needs?

Amber: Yes, that sounds great. I'm just looking at my calendar now, and I know it's short notice, but Darren will be in the office tomorrow. Could we meet then?

Me: The sooner we get this sorted, the better. I'll prepare a tailored strategy and market analysis to ensure your salary packages are competitive. Thanks so much for taking the time to chat today.

What Felt Different About this Conversation?

On the surface, this looks like a long conversation, but it flowed as easily as a brew with a mate who finally admits they're in over their head. We didn't swoop in with "super recruiter" energy. We didn't tear into the job description like it was an IKEA manual. We didn't even mention "candidates" until Amber had talked herself into a small existential crisis.

Instead, we walked her through her world, her workload, her blind spots, her internal politics and that charming cocktail of tight deadlines and tighter budgets. The questions weren't clever; they were simply the right ones, asked at the right time, until Amber realised she didn't need a recruiter... she needed a lifeline.

By the time we reached expectations, she wasn't asking whether she should use an agency; she was laying out the criteria for the one she wanted.

That's the beauty of the Triple E approach: you don't convince anyone; you let them in, and this does the heavy lifting.

Amber didn't feel sold to, pushed or pressured. She felt supported, clearer and partnered. That's why this works. That's the real game.

Reflection: Building Trust, Changing the Game

Across all three conversations, the same foundation carried us through:

A mindset focused on curiosity, not control.
Questions designed to help them think, not trap them into buying.
A primary objective of building trust, not extracting jobs.

When we approach prospects and clients this way, something powerful happens: they lower their guard, start thinking aloud and take ownership of their challenges, inviting us in to help.

No forced rapport, sales desperation or endless rejection loops. Just honest conversations that create real opportunities, naturally and cleanly.

If rejection has been your norm and flaky prospects have been your frustration, take a deep breath, because what you've just seen isn't a new trick; it's a new perspective.

A better way to connect, sell and recruit.

Job Intake next. Bring snacks.

Client Rap-Up

Spam to Slam

Yo, we flicked the switch, rewired the chat
No more “You recruiting?” We’re better than that.
No pitch-slaps, no PSL dreams,
Just real talk flowin’ through the outreach streams.

"Not hiring?” Fine, we plant the seed,
Next time they struggle, they know who they need.
So if you’re still blastin’ from your CRM,
You’re looking more cringey than a salesy DM.

This ain’t recruitment like back in the day,
It’s facilitation that paves the way.
From cold call chill, warming it through

Prospect respect the **Clean Soul Crew.**

Chapter 7

Job Intake

Cracking the Brief Before it Breaks You

Oh, the sweet smell of a new vacancy.

A brand-new job brief lands on your desk. A glance at the job title and responsibilities, and for a glorious moment, everything feels possible. You can already hear the ka-ching of commission jingling somewhere in the distance, and you're picturing yourself moonwalking out of the office at month-end. Then reality barges in, wearing steel-capped boots:

The client vanishes into the witness protection programme.
The "urgent" role is now gathering dust.
The job description reads like it was written during a hostage situation.
The salary's so low you'd need to pay someone in magic beans.
Let's not even mention the Glassdoor reviews.

Welcome to the glamorous recruitment life, where jobs are plentiful and genuinely fillable roles are rarer than a retained brief with no hidden landmines.

The trick to survival (and, dare we say, success) isn't just in finding candidates faster. It's about spotting the potholes ahead before your recruitment process blows a tyre.

The Real Problem Is Never Just the Vacancy

Every unfilled job is like a crime scene: the job description is just the blood spatter. The real story is buried. We call these hidden tripwires Blind Spots.

No client tells you these upfront (sometimes because they don't even realise them themselves), like: the role is a political football. The budget approval is "pending" (translation: "non-existent"). The hiring manager and HR are quietly at war. The last three people who took this role visibly aged under the strain.

When we fail to investigate what's happening during this stage, we fall into the trap of thinking every job can be fixed by flinging more CVs. That's how we end up with a pipeline full of "maybe" candidates and a whiteboard full of broken dreams. However, when we focus on discovering the true purpose of the job, what they need a new hire to address, and what is hiding in their baggage, everything changes. You stop being "another agency." You become an advisor, a partner, and a fixer of the hidden mess.

Storytime: The Curious Case of the Sabotaged Sales Manager

Some years back, I got a call from a small manufacturing company. Their MD practically demanded that I come "immediately" to take on a Sales Manager vacancy.

When I arrived, it felt less like a briefing and more like a kidnapping. For the first hour, he ranted about hopeless candidates, disappointing recruiters, and, for good measure, how dismal everyone under 40 was. No vision for the role, no passion for the company, just a rolling monologue of moaning and misery.

Halfway through, I'd had enough. I stood up, gathered my things, and said, "It doesn't sound like I'm the right person to help you." Stunned, he told me to sit back down. He apologised, and this is where the dynamics changed. I asked him, "What's really going on here?" Boom. Turns out, the real issue wasn't the candidates or the recruiters. It was him.

He was past retirement age, his wife wanted him to retire, and he wasn't ready to let go. Whenever a half-decent candidate appeared, he subconsciously found reasons to reject them. We talked honestly about the impact on his marriage, health, and business. I offered to support him in whatever way he needed. A few hours later, he called me back, ready to move forward. I filled the role within two weeks.

Lesson? The "vacancy" was never the problem. The Blind Spot was.

Ego: The Silent Assassin of a Job Intake

There are two main reasons recruiters don't dig deeply enough into the job specs that land in their inboxes.

The first is fear.

The thought of uncovering information that might point to the role being genuinely unfillable can feel uncomfortable. After all, we might get lucky. We might find a candidate. We might be the hero. So, we take our chances, especially in a market that's light on jobs and heavy on pressure.

The second reason is ego.

It steps in and reminds us that we're the industry experts. We've filled hundreds of similar roles before. So, we rush to reassure: "I've got this. You're in safe hands. Leave it with me."

We avoid asking too many questions because we don't want to look like we haven't got a clue. Somewhere along the line, curiosity starts to feel like a downgrade, as though asking questions cancels out credibility.

So, we fill in the gaps, rely on pattern recognition, and hope it all holds up.

That isn't expertise; it's assumption dressed up as confidence.

The reality is this:

- Every job we work on has a very unique DNA, challenges, and blind spots.

- Every hiring manager operates under a unique set of decision-making criteria.
- Every business or organisation has a unique set of stakeholders lurking in the background with conflicting agendas.

When we shy away from discovering what sits beneath the surface, those things don't disappear. They resurface later, usually after we've already invested time, energy, and credibility.

When we put our ego back in the snack drawer, we're not losing authority; we are gaining something far more valuable. We become a partner and a genuine stakeholder in the hiring process.

The Clean Soul Job Intake in Action

In the next section, we're going to walk through how to do a real, clean-soul job intake, using one live example that shows you how to:

Explore the job role in more detail.
Evaluate the skills and expertise needed in the role.
Align and manage expectations.
Position ourselves as a true recruitment partner (not a CV slinger).

Questions to Avoid

When it comes to job briefings, the questions we ask matter just as much as they do with prospects. Too often, recruiters fall back on the routine ones: safe, predictable, and usually no more revealing than the job description itself. At best, they make us sound like we're filling out a form; at worst, they confirm the client's suspicion that we're only there to "get the spec" rather than understand the role in depth.

We're often told we should be asking the tougher questions here, the ones that challenge, that push back on the realities of the role.

But how? What do those questions actually look like? Which ones push them to recoil and brace, and which draw them in so they can see the truth of the job for themselves? Too often, instead of guiding them with the right questions, we default to "educating" them, and this isn't the same as discovery; one has us doing all the talking, the other helps them see it for themselves.

AVOID: What does the job entail?
REPLACE: What difference do you need someone to make in this role?

AVOID: What is the salary range for this role?
REPLACE: How will you decide between the cost of the right talent and your current internal pay structure?

AVOID: How quickly do you need to fill this role?
REPLACE: How are you currently covering the gap without anyone in this role?

AVOID: What are the must-have skills you are looking for in a candidate?
REPLACE: How will you distinguish between the skills that are crucial to the role and those that you might be able to teach or support?

AVOID: What is the reason for this role?
REPLACE: What impact would not filling this role have on the business?

AVOID: Who else is involved in the interview process?
REPLACE: How will you align the different priorities of the stakeholders involved to reach a unanimous decision on a hire?

With those reframes in place, let's step into a real intake conversation and see how the right questions, mindset, and building trust uncover far more than a job description ever could.

The Job Intake Conversation

We are following up on the scenario from the previous chapter, where we discussed a first call with a new client seeking help to find skilled, technically biased staff.

A quick word on the names you'll come across here: the people are not real. I simply lifted the first name I spotted in my LinkedIn feed on the day I was writing. Company names were also invented, just in case you are frantically stalking them. If one of them does exist somewhere out there, then apologies in advance... pure coincidence, not a recruitment sting.

After the initial call, I visited the company and met with Darren, the Head of the PMH division, and Amber, the HR Manager. My goal was to learn more about them, explore the candidate landscape, and determine whether we could collaborate to hire the right people.

The company is Nordalyn, a mid-sized engineering firm based in the UK, with its head office and manufacturing plant in Denmark. They have seven sales offices worldwide. They specialise in maintenance tech that helps manufacturers reduce downtime, mainly in the automotive, plastics, and aerospace sectors. However, they have recently branched into something new: an innovative system designed specifically for the food processing industry, called the ProActive Maintenance Hub (PMH). They've poured a small fortune into this product's launch. It's all bells, whistles, and predictive algorithms that make engineers swoon.

All they need now is a UK team to drive it forward.

Enter Darren. He's sent me a job description for a Technical Sales Engineer that reads like a cross between a wish list and a bedtime story from the late 1990s: lengthy, rigid, and packed with "must-haves." They've agreed to be flexible on salary and signed the Terms of Business. I pitched for a retained search, and they countered with a one-month exclusive. Fair play.

Before we dive in, this is where the real work begins. Job descriptions are rarely the truth, the whole truth, and nothing but the truth. They're more like the glossy trailer to a film that turns out to have a very different plot. So before I start searching for candidates who don't actually exist, we need to peel back the layers, get under the skin of the brief, and work out what story we're really telling here and what Darren actually needs rather than what he's scribbled in the "ideal world" column.

Exploration: From the JD to the Real Story

The objective of this stage is to identify any underlying needs and gather more information about the job, enabling me to package and present it effectively to potential candidates.

Commentary:
I have already gone through the key responsibilities and expectations for the role with him, so our conversation starts with me summarising this:

Me: Just to clarify the key points of the job. You're looking for a Technical Salesperson selling a predictive maintenance system to food processors throughout the UK. It's a new business role, ideally suited for a candidate based in the Midlands. Given the market conditions, you are flexible on salary and willing to pay up to a £65k base, and commission, which could realistically give them another £30k a year. Have I got that right?

Darren: Yes, that's about right.

Me: What has made this particular role a priority for you right now?

Darren: It's critical to the launch of this product. We've got a ton of leads coming through for the PMH system, but we can't get through them.

Commentary:
It's like discovering a treasure chest full of gold, but the key is just out

of reach, or worse, locked in a cabinet, and someone at head office forgot the combination.

Me: That must be putting some pressure on your sales pipeline. What's driving these leads coming in?

Darren: Our head office has been running global marketing campaigns. The system has already proven to reduce downtime and save on breakdown costs, so it's gaining a lot of traction; people are contacting us from all over.

Commentary:
At our meeting, we delved into the nitty-gritty of the product. This isn't just another maintenance system; it's a poster child for predictive maintenance. Fully integrated, customisable, sexy tech with sensors smart enough to spot a problem before the operator does. It's the engineering version of a sixth sense. It's been designed specifically for the food processing industry.

Me: It's rare to hear of a business struggling to manage an avalanche of leads. How are you and your team currently dealing with this?

Darren: It's mostly me, plus two others covering our usual sectors. However, none of us is familiar with the food industry, so properly pushing anything through is challenging. We just don't have the capacity or specialist knowledge.

Me: It must be frustrating to have a product that almost sells itself, but no one to close the deal with.

Commentary:
It's like having a Ferrari in the driveway, but no one has a licence to drive it.

Darren: Exactly. Germany and the United States have already launched and smashed the hell out of their targets. We're behind simply because we don't have a focused team in place. It's not the products fault.

Commentary:
They're practically printing money across the pond, but in the UK, they are stuck playing catch-up with a slingshot while the other countries are firing cannons.

Me: That's a great selling point for potential candidates: success in other regions, strong product, loads of opportunity here in the UK. What would you be looking for this person to achieve in this role?

Darren: Around £1.5 million in their first year, and as we are sitting on a potential bank of leads worth over £800k, that should be a piece of cake. What we really need is someone who can open the doors to some of the biggest food processors. Oh, and wiping the smug smile off my counterpart's face in Germany and America would be the icing on the cake.

Me: That sounds reasonable. How long have you been looking to fill this particular role?

Darren: About 3 months now, give or take.

Commentary:
Come on, Darren; 3 months and no success? You have a cupboard full of ignored leads; it's not a pipeline issue; it's a people one.

Me: That's quite a while. What do you think has prevented you from finding the right fit?

Darren: I think it's probably been down to the market. We didn't realise it was so bad, and the fact that we were trying to do it on a shoestring didn't help either.

Me: Yes, I think it's been quite an eye-opener for you, and I'm so pleased to see you having a different view and more salary flexibility. Before we move on to the type of person you're looking for, it seems that this role has a compelling story: a market-ready product, huge lead potential, real earnings, and career-defining opportunities. Is there anything else I should include when I'm talking to candidates?

Darren: They'll be shaping the division from scratch. Complete training, investment in R&D, and a great bonus. This could be a step into a director-level role if they're good.

Exploration Summary

We now have a clear and compelling picture of what this role offers, not just a list of duties, but a genuine opportunity with substance behind it. By digging beneath the job description, we've uncovered the elements that matter to candidates: impact, earnings, growth, and the chance to shape something from the ground up. That gives us everything we need to craft a job advert that gets noticed, and more importantly, we are now in a position to sell a vision that candidates can believe in.

Evaluation: Candidate Requirements

During this stage, the focus will be on determining the type of candidate who would most likely meet their needs. Looking at the job specification, he will not have a prayer in hell of getting all his boxes checked, so I will have my work cut out for me in opening this up. We will also examine the potential obstacles he is likely to encounter and explore how he plans to overcome them.

Commentary:
We've nailed the job specifics, but unless we can find someone to do the job, it's all academic. This part of the call is where Darren's dreams of a magical, ready-made candidate come up against the cold, hard light of reality. My job here isn't to rain on his parade, just to help him realise the marching band he's waiting for probably doesn't exist.

Me: Looking at your candidate specification, I can see the four main points: at least 5 years of proven technical sales ability, experience selling maintenance systems and selling these into the food processing sector, as well as having an engineering qualification. What do you think the demand is like for all these skills?

Darren: Judging by our response so far to the adverts, I think it's pretty tight. I just don't understand it.

Commentary:
Tighter than a duck's arse, mate, and that's being generous. The real issue here isn't just supply; it's expectation.

Me: Yes, there is significant demand for candidates like these. If there isn't anyone out there who ticks all your boxes, what's the impact of leaving this role unfilled for much longer?

Darren: I don't want to think about it. We're already starting to lose ground. If this carries on, we'll end up missing the market altogether. It'll look like the UK just couldn't deliver. Are you saying you won't be able to find someone?

Me: Considering I need to meet all the criteria, I think it will take longer to find someone. Where do you think the candidates with the experience you need are currently working?

Darren: More than likely, our competitors. [He mentions three main big players.] It would be great if we could get someone from one of them. Do you think you can recruit people from there?

Commentary:
Ah, the classic plan: "Let's just steal someone perfect from a market leader and hope they'll happily jump ship." The confidence is admirable, but the realism... less so. At the meeting, we discussed the company's competition. They were huge, well-known players in the industry and several rungs up the food chain from them. Candidates with the needed skills are more inclined to want to work for a prestigious organisation with a certain amount of kudos.

Me: I can certainly approach these people, but how much bargaining power would you have in getting them to leave a well-paid role, an established customer base, and the kudos of working for an industry leader?

Darren: As you know, we can be flexible with the package, and they would be able to bring their accounts and service them with a much better product. I reckon some people might want to work for someone who isn't as rigid or inflexible as some big players. We have a great environment that would enable you to grow into a senior or director-level role much more quickly.

Commentary:
To be fair, it's not a bad pitch. However, what he's describing is a fantasy candidate who has both the motivation to leave and zero loyalty to their current employer; those get snapped up quickly, usually by people who act on their interest without a three-month gap between interest and action.

Me: You have a pioneering product that would seem attractive to potential candidates. If you were to acquire someone from one of your competitors, what consequences might you face in retaining their existing customers?

Darren: I guess most of the accounts would be under contract, so there might be some complications, but I'm sure we could overcome that, as our product can integrate with whatever system a customer has.

Commentary:
"And by overcome, I mean ignore completely and hope no one sues us." Right?

Me: How would you minimise the risk of one of your competitors countering your offer or another of them head-hunting the candidate out of your company?

Darren: I'm unsure; I didn't think it was that cutthroat out there. But there again, it stands to reason that they will only try to nick them back again. That isn't something we can afford to do. You're the recruiter; what would you suggest?

Commentary:
This is the moment you wait for, when the "market conditions" excuse turns into an honest reflection. Darren's starting to realise that hiring in this climate isn't about budget or job ads. It's about

understanding what good looks like today, not what it looked like ten years ago.

Me: I think we need to open the spec up more. I understand it's vital for the person to have experience selling in the food industry. How important is having engineering qualifications and experience in maintenance systems?

Darren: Well, their route to market and sales ability are non-negotiables. I guess having an engineering qualification isn't the be-all and end-all, as long as they have some technical knowledge. However, we need someone who can hit the ground running, so having experience in maintenance systems would be key.

Commentary:
Progress. Not a complete U-turn, but the satnav is at least recalculating.

Me: I understand. How long do you imagine it would take someone with experience in selling another technical product into the food industry to understand your system?

Darren: It would depend on the product. If it were processing or automation equipment, then not long, I suppose. When they start the role, we will send them off to Denmark for two weeks to get training on our product anyway, so I think this should equip them with the knowledge they need.

Me: That's great. I didn't realise they would be getting that. Apart from maintenance systems, what other products could they have sold?

Darren: Let's see. Robotics, mixing and check-weighing products, gas control systems, burners, X-ray systems, metal detectors, packaging systems, and conveyors. Things like ingredients, though, wouldn't be relevant.

Me: Thank you. That will open up the search and give you more options without the legal implications of stealing someone else's database. So, just to clarify, you're okay with considering candidates who have sold technical products into the food processing industry, even if they don't have an engineering qualification or experience in maintenance systems. Is that right?

Darren: Yes, opening it up makes sense as long as they have the right contacts.

Me: I understand how critical it is that they can open the right doors for you. How have you been assessing the applicants' CVs you have received?

Darren: I generally like to see what they've sold and who they know in the industry.

Me: Since most salespeople don't put their treasured contacts on a CV, how would you know if they were worth getting in for an interview?

Darren: That's a good point, I suppose. We've likely overlooked some qualified candidates, as we've been relying solely on job applications. Is that something you can establish when you speak to them?

Commentary:
At this point, it starts to feel like pulling teeth, not because Darren's unwilling, but because every shift in thinking has to be earned. But that's the work. The more he talks, the more he starts to see the gap between what he's asking for and how he will get it. That's the moment we need.

Me: Yes, I can. What else would you need me to establish to feel confident that you would want to interview them?

Darren: We would need to know the types of products they have sold. What have they achieved against the target? How many customers have they won? What food processing plants do they deal with? What's their average deal size?

Me: Is there anything else that would make you say, "Wow, I want to see them today?"

Darren: Definitely, if they have sold to larger food processors with an average order value of £200k, especially if they have sold maintenance systems before.

Commentary:
We've gone from "must tick every box" to "let's open it up." That might not sound like much, but that's a bloody breakthrough in recruiter land. Darren's still holding onto a few non-negotiables, but we've chipped away at the concrete and found some flexibility. More importantly, we've identified the risks: delays, counteroffers, and overestimating candidate availability without ever implying that he is being unrealistic. That's the art.

Now, with the specification slightly looser and expectations of the candidate market more aligned, it's time to discuss how this process will run and how we keep good candidates engaged once we've found them.

Before we move forward, this is the moment to tighten the bolts. Exploration gave us the "what" and Evaluation exposed the "why." Expectations is more the how. It's where good intentions collide with timelines, stakeholders, and the candidate experience, the stuff that makes or breaks a placement long before an offer letter ever gets sent.

To get this right, we need to look at how Darren plans to show up in the process, what he'll need from me, and how we prevent the usual potholes that trip up even the strongest searches. This is where alignment becomes momentum.

Expectations: Alignment

This section focuses on how Darren plans to attract, evaluate, and retain suitable candidates throughout the process, aligning expectations with reality rather than fantasy. It's where good intentions meet the hiring plan.

Me: Based on what we discussed in our meeting about candidates being in high demand, minimising the risks of counteroffers whilst enhancing the candidate experience, what might you do differently during the interview stage?

Darren: Good question. I suppose I'll be more enthusiastic and get the message across about the role's potential. I'll come across as more excited about the product, the company, and the growth path. I'll also make sure to ask better questions, moving beyond the usual "tell me about a time" stuff.

Me: That sounds like a great start. How confident do you feel about doing interviews?

Darren: I hate them. I struggle to think on my feet and often forget what I need to ask.

Me: That is more common than you think. What support would you need to craft relevant interview questions?

Darren: What, you can do that? That would be a massive help!

Commentary:
He's gone from trying harder to asking for help, a subtle but critical shift. Confidence doesn't come from pretending you've got it covered. It comes from getting the proper support and knowing you're not winging it.

Me: I'll send you some. How do you plan to fit in interviews around your busy workload and travel?

Darren: The first one will be over Teams, so I could fit those in to suit the candidate. If I believe they are worth setting up a face-to-face, we will ensure this happens quickly, within a week. Given our understanding of the market, we will also accommodate people outside of regular hours. I'm pretty flexible with that.

Commentary:
Classic. When people are unsure how to change a process, they often promise to smile more and try harder. It's sincere, but not a strategy.

Me: That's excellent news. I've known many candidates who have been snapped up if there are delays in the process. What would you need to establish in the interview to feel confident that they would fit in with your culture?

Darren: Erm, it's going to be a gut feeling more than anything. I will try to find out what they are passionate about and how driven they are. Wait, I've just had an idea.

Me: (laughs) Wow, I'm all ears, go for it.

Darren: What if we offered the candidate a quick video call with one of our salespeople in Germany or the US? They're already flying with this product; they could give the candidate a real-world view of what it's like out there. Not from us. From someone already doing the job. First-hand. Honest. Unfiltered. What do you think? Is it a bit unorthodox?

Me: That's genius. Totally unexpected, and smart. It shows that you have nothing to hide and everything to be proud of. That kind of peer insight builds belief. Would you be able to arrange that?

Darren: I've got to speak to them, obviously, but I can't see any problem with that. The candidate would be able to ask them anything they wanted.

Commentary:
Well, I wasn't expecting that. A cracking idea, and from Darren, no less. The man I'd pegged as a bit stuck in his ways just leap-frogged half the market with one flash of insight. My perception of him is changing by the second. He isn't just cooperating now, he is co-creating, and that's when you know they're in.

Me: Once we've presented a strong candidate, how quickly would you be looking to move through the process and make a decision?

Darren: If I like them, I'd want to move fast. I don't want to drag this out and risk losing someone good.

Me: Great. Is there anyone else involved in signing off on the final hire?

Darren: Yes, the board of Directors in our head office. They won't be involved in the interview, but they will want a summary and a recommendation before I formally make the offer.

Me: Got it. So, giving them a heads-up earlier in the process will help avoid delays later.

Darren: Exactly.

Me: What needs to be in place before this person joins in terms of onboarding?

Darren: Amber generally handles all that stuff. They'll need a home office set-up, a laptop, a phone, a car, a CRM licence, and a proper introduction to our sales structure. She will also have to book the product training in Denmark. I'll speak with Amber to ensure that's all sorted in advance.

Me: Perfect. How do you want me to present potential candidates to you?

Darren: I would like a summary, and the CV would be great. It should include key points on why you're recommending them, experience, contacts, and achievements. Bullet points are fine; I don't need War and Peace. If you're unsure about someone, please call and discuss it with Amber or me.

Me: Noted. And when you've received a candidate from me, how soon can I expect feedback?

Darren: I'll do my best to respond within 24 hours. I'll let you know if I need more time, but I want to keep the momentum, so I'll prioritise it.

Commentary:
This is where the rubber meets the road. No vague promises; just clear expectations on both sides. Speed, structure, and mutual accountability. The flash of inspiration was brilliant, and this is where trust is built. When Darren commits to timely feedback, prepares internally, and agrees on how candidates will be reviewed, that's

when you know the partnership is genuine. He's no longer just a hiring manager. He's a collaborator.

Next Steps

Me: Thanks, Darren. That gives me everything I need. Based on our discussion, I'll write a new advert that reflects the real opportunity here, not just duties, but the story, the growth, and the impact. I'll send you a copy for approval before it goes live.

Darren: Sounds good.

Me: In the meantime, I'll start the search, focusing on candidates who can open doors, bring the right relationships, and thrive in this kind of environment. If someone stands out, you'll be the first to know. You should receive the first profiles within the week. Do you want me to copy anyone else into the email chain?

Darren: Yes, copy Amber into everything. Probably have a chat with her regarding the interview questions.

Me: I will. It might be worth pitching your idea to the salespeople in Germany and America to ensure they would be happy to chat with candidates. This is a brilliant idea, by the way.

Darren: I've surprised myself with it. I will catch up with them today.

Me: Thank you so much for your time today and for letting me bend your ear. I'm very excited about getting this show on the road.

Commentary:
And there it is, the handshake moment, not in ink, but in intent. This isn't just about sourcing a candidate. It's about building a recruitment partnership where trust flows in both directions. Darren's onboard, open, and ready. Now the real work begins.

Summary

This call charts the transformation of Darren, from an old-school, spec-driven hiring manager stuck in a "We've always done it this way" mindset, to someone genuinely engaged in shaping a stand-out candidate experience. That was no mean feat, but we have a genuine shot now at filling the role.

There was one question I didn't cover in this script:

"Who do you already have in the business who could potentially be trained to do this job?"

The reason I didn't ask it here is because it had already been explored. Darren had explained how the role was currently being covered and the lack of anyone internally with food processing experience. That said, I recommend you ask this question in every job intake you do.

They will almost always have considered it anyway, so you're not putting ideas into their heads. What it does do is give you clarity on what's already been tried, and it significantly reduces that end-of-process conversation that starts with: "Sorry, we went with an internal candidate." We've all been there.

Job Advert

Well, we've reached that moment. We've had the intake conversation, gathered all the information we need, and now come to the bit that many of us dread the most.

Putting together a job advert.

It's time-consuming, it drains whatever creative energy we've got left in the day, and it often comes with the added pressure of being first to market. Many recruiters have stopped bothering altogether. Why waste time crafting an advert that will mostly attract irrelevant applications when you could just get on with the search?

(By the way, there is a way to cope with "application overload" that will be covered in Chapter 9.)

So instead, we slap a few prompts into ChatGPT, paste in the job description, and hey presto... a publishable advert. Job done.

Except that candidates can spot these a mile off and don't take them seriously. Why should they?

Even if you never publish a job advert publicly, you still need something credible and tangible to show to passive candidates. Something that reassures them the role is real, thought through, and worth their time. You don't want the market wondering whether you're talking about a "maybe job" or a role that only exists in your head.

A good job advert isn't really about advertising or over-selling. It's about orientation.

It gives candidates a reason to lean in. It helps them understand why the role exists, what problem it's there to solve, and whether it's a move that makes sense for them. Done well, it doesn't try to persuade; it allows the right people to recognise themselves.

This is where the relationship with the job really matters.

If you've rushed the intake, relied on a recycled job description, or avoided the uncomfortable questions, it will show immediately. A compelling advert can't exist without a proper discovery call or intake meeting, because the quality of the advert is a direct reflection of the quality of the conversation that came before it.

The example that follows is built from the intake call with Darren, not the job description.

Not everything that could have gone into this advert has been included. That is deliberate. The aim is to say enough for the right people to recognise whether this role is worth their attention.

While many recruiters now bypass job boards altogether, it's worth remembering that adverts can still surface people you'd never think to search for: those who've recently relocated, been made redundant, or simply had one difficult conversation too many.

Technical Sales Engineer – Food Processing (UK)

Base: £65k + £30k OTE, paid quarterly Work from a home base covering the UK territory

---

Why this role is worth a look

A global manufacturer of maintenance systems has developed a predictive maintenance solution designed for food processing environments, where hygiene, uptime, and production risk drive buying decisions. Sales offices in other regions are already converting enquiries into revenue using this solution. The UK launch is underway. Enquiries are coming in, but there is currently no one in the UK team with food processing experience to qualify, progress, and close them. This role exists to change that.

The Remit:

- Converting inbound leads into sales opportunities
- Opening conversations with larger food processors and progressing deals through multiple stakeholders

About you

- You understand how buying decisions are made in food processing environments and how operational constraints influence purchasing behaviour.
- You've sold capital equipment rather than off-the-shelf products, such as maintenance systems, robotics, automation, processing machinery, inspection equipment, or similar.

If you recognise yourself in that description and want to represent a product that food manufacturers recognise as addressing real operational problems...let's get the ball rolling.

Intake Rap-Up

The Reset Session

Yo, JD dropped heavy, list long as a scroll,
Darren wanted unicorns to fill the hole.
Spec so rigid, market so thin,
Even Harry Potter couldn't magic one in.

We dug past the bluster, slipped through the crack,
Faced the blind spots he'd shoved out back.
Then mid-chat twist, man drops a gem,
"Let the Yanks talk real, give the pitch to them."

Didn't see it coming, fair play to the bloke,
One brilliant idea, and the old frame broke.
Now feedback's tight, HR's in the loop,
No lone-wolf vibes, we roll as a troop.

From VHS specs to a Netflix plan,
That's a vacancy reset... **Clean Soul stand.**

Chapter 8

The AI Candidate Takeover Bid

Candidate.exe: System Failure

Suppose AI vendors started selling their agentic software as a business development weapon, something that could missile-lock onto the right prospects, charm them, handle objections, sense hesitation and walk away with a signed job spec. In that case, we'd all be buying licences faster than you can say pipeline drought. Skint or not, we'd find the budget.

But we all know it's not within its capability. That would require sentient AI, and that isn't even in its embryonic stage yet.

Winning business isn't a pattern-matching task. It requires persuasion, timing, intuition, social awareness, reading subtext, evaluating conflicting signals, judging risk, calibrating tone and building trust with people who often don't want to trust you in the first place. It's messy, emotional and political work, and no AI system is equipped for that.

It still needs a human or two.

This is where the recruitment dynamics split. On the client side, AI can't get close to the real work of relationships, so it doesn't even try.

But on the candidate side? That's where it sinks its teeth in. Relationships apparently don't enter the equation. It's just structured data, keywords, forms and funnel optimisation. Quick, clean, high-volume, low-risk and very easy for software companies to automate and monetise.

So instead of one connected hiring ecosystem, we now have a

lopsided one. Clients get humans. Candidates get machines.

That imbalance, one could even call it bias, is already reshaping the entire candidate experience, for better, for worse and for whatever comes next.

The Candidate Experience

Ahh, remember that phrase? It was on every recruiter's lips during the war on talent in 2021 to 2022, back in the days when we were drowning in jobs and turning some away because we didn't have the bandwidth.

The so-called "Great Resignation" quickly turned into the "Great Hesitation." Suddenly no one wanted to move. You couldn't find candidates for love nor money. We pampered them, protected them and went out on a limb for them.

For a brief, shining moment in recruitment's history, the candidate was royalty.

Now those days feel like folklore. The tide has turned. Jobs have fallen off a cliff and the crown has slipped. They're the ones scrambling for footing and it's become the "candidate what?"

So let's take a peek at what the candidate market is dealing with now. The word chaos doesn't come anywhere near close.

Today's job seeker is expected to navigate a gauntlet of rules, warnings, contradictions and best practices, most of which we've thrown at them in a panic while trying to reverse-engineer what the algorithms want.

One day it's remove the green banner, it looks desperate. The next day it's keep the green banner, it boosts visibility.

We tell them to:

Network constantly
Create a personal brand

Post content on LinkedIn every day
Comment on thought leaders' posts
Tailor your CV to each job
Use keywords
Show personality but maintain professionalism
Highlight achievements
Quantify results
Align cultural fit

We push all this onto people who simply came to the job market for one reason: to keep a roof over their heads. Most job seekers are not influencers, marketeers, SEO specialists or brand managers. They're people whose industries never required them to perform like dancing monkeys for employment until now.

Is it any wonder they're confused, overwhelmed, suspicious and, frankly, pissed off with us?

From the candidate's perspective, it looks like we are no longer the bridge. We're the obstacle. The gatekeepers of a game they never signed up to play, and that's before we get to the scammers who have swooped in to exploit the chaos:

Offering guaranteed ATS optimisation
Fake jobs posted as bait
£200+ CV keywording packages for roles that don't exist
Confidence tricks dressed up as career advice

Desperate candidates are paying for fixes to problems they shouldn't have to solve in the first place, so they start gaming the system themselves.

AI-generated CVs
AI-generated interview answers
Inflated keywords
Fictional achievements
Profiles redesigned for algorithms instead of the truth

And there we are, calling them out on LinkedIn. It's becoming us-versus-them, and by doing so, we're only driving ourselves deeper into reputational rot.

They are not being unethical. Desperate times call for desperate measures as they try to survive a system that feels rigged against them. They're reacting to the experience, the one shaped by rushed processes, conflicting advice, broken expectations and automation that treats them like data before anyone treats them like humans.

That is the heart of the problem. AI didn't break the candidate experience; it exposed how fragile it already was.

If the candidate side wasn't fraught enough, we've now entered a phase where even we don't fully understand the ground we're standing on. One job posting can attract three hundred applications, with half arriving in the first hour. Some are human, some are AI-generated and some are gold buried under formatting that an algorithm will never read properly. Recruiters are staring at piles of data, not people, and no one can say with confidence what's slipping through the cracks.

Every single one of us is winging it.

It's easy to point the finger at AI and blame it for the havoc it's caused by stealing the candidate-facing parts of the process.

AI is not at fault. It's the market, the economy, a hiring environment stitched together with hesitation, budget freezes, fear of risk, longer sign-offs and companies that want exceptional talent but can't justify the spend.

It's a perfect storm that none of us caused or can control, and it's simply arrived, full of promises but without an instruction manual.

We all know that it can lighten the workload, absorb volume we cannot physically manage, but it cannot calm a terrified market, change skittish hiring managers or force decisions that businesses are afraid to make. It absolutely cannot rescue good people falling through the cracks because their CV didn't hit the right keywords on the right day at the right moment.

The irony is that AI is still in its toddler stage, clumsy, enthusiastic and unpredictable. It's learning how to run and knocking things down everywhere it goes.

Love it or hate it, we can't denounce it. It's here to stay and it will get better, but only if we teach it what better actually looks like. Without guidance, it's just pattern-matching inside a tornado and hoping for the best.

So no, Artificial Intelligence isn't the villain here. It didn't create the broken dynamics. It magnified what was already cracking under pressure.

Full Circle

Here's where it loops back on itself. It might not be something we want to hear, but we laid the groundwork for all of this.

We didn't lose the candidate experience overnight. It was eroded, bit by bit, at our own hands. Now, in a hiring landscape that feels like purgatory with a dashboard, we are scrambling to stay relevant while the market watches us, clients and candidates alike, and asks a question we have spent years dodging:

What value are we adding?

This is the reckoning. The moment when the old-school approach finally withers on contact.

The Clean Soul Way Forward

The only way we are going to claw our way out of this chaos is to eradicate our old attitude towards candidates completely. That legacy playbook has caused more foundational damage than most of us will ever fully comprehend. Agentic AI has simply leaned into it and is building on it, and we can all see how that is playing out.

- We have to cultivate a new, genuine way of perceiving candidates.
- We have to recognise them as an embedded, integral element of the recruitment dynamic.
- We have to take responsibility for ensuring they feel valued at our hands, even when we cannot help them.

When we understand that, everything else falls into place. The machines will learn. We will be able to work alongside them, letting them take the heavy lifting while we work toward the same objective: creating a healthier, more human candidate experience.

I want to be crystal clear here. This isn't just about being nicer to candidates. A new mindset that pursues candidate excellence does not require anyone to become an obsequious, arse-licking sycophant.

However, it does require something far harder: taking responsibility for repairing what we broke.

That begins in the next chapter.

Candidate Armageddon next: Bring that slightly suspect can at the back of the fridge with neon liquid inside and a flavour that legally shouldn't exist.

The AI Rap-Up

Hit the Road, Stack

Hit the road, Stack, your reign is hack,
Clean Soul, Clean Soul, Clean Soul, Clean Soul,
Hit the road, Stack, we're taking back control, Clean Soul.

AI, AI, you're runnin' wild today,
Don't go treatin' candidates that way.
You scrape a little data then you churn out a match,
But you're copyin' old habits that belong in the trash.

You're sortin', you're filterin', like it's all just a game,
While the humans underneath it take the weight and the blame.
We see the mess buildin' in the funnel each day,
And the scammers circlin' round in a predatory way.

The panic, the pressure, the noise in the feed,
The quick-fix illusions no one actually needs.
You may just be an AI tool,
But I'm lettin' you know that I ain't no fool.
Give up the ghost, 'Cause **Clean Souls** still rule.

Chapter 9

Candidate Armageddon

The Barometer of our Reputation

What if candidates aren't the problem at all?
What if they're the profit...
And we're just the bloody overhead?

For decades, we've refused to acknowledge our attitude towards candidates. We've treated them as noise, admin, and the third wheel wedged between us and a fee.

Now we're seeing the results at scale: disengagement, distrust, and our reputation bleeding out in public. Look at the posts, look at the anger: candidates don't believe a word we say, they see us as ghosters, time-wasters, and opportunists, and are struggling to differentiate us from the scammers and fakery out there.

If we're being honest with ourselves, this didn't come out of nowhere. We've always loved having a good old whinge about candidates: How they lie to us, let us down, apply to everything that moves, and then expect us to manage their careers, their notice periods and emotional well-being.

For years, that narrative has been recycled so often it's become an accepted, convenient truth. It's far easier to blame them than to examine how our own behaviours, systems, and pressures have shaped the experience on the other side of the inbox.

Unfortunately, we're no longer playing to the same audience.

Today's candidates are more informed, vocal, and far less willing to tolerate being treated as expendable. They now have a platform and are publicly and loudly calling out poor practice, without apology. Ghosting, and transactional behaviour aren't just being noticed, they're being documented.

Whether we agree with them or not is irrelevant. The perception is already out there, and this is where the real divide appears.

I recently came across two LinkedIn posts, almost back-to-back, from recruitment founders working in niche markets. Their views on the candidate landscape couldn't have been more polarising. The first one I'm going to summarise is a perfect example of the legacy mindset holding on for dear life.

Post One:

This was positioned as an "educational" message to candidates, essentially a justification for why most applications are ignored.

The author explained that much of the frustration candidates feel stems from a misunderstanding of how recruitment works. In her view, because companies pay recruiters, the primary responsibility is to meet the client's expectations, not to support every individual who applies. Rejection, she suggested, is rarely personal; it simply reflects the client's defined criteria. She also noted that although many recruiters *would like* to help more job seekers, it's not realistic given the workload and the commercial priorities of the role. She also mentioned that we are not career coaches, but we often get mistaken for being one.

My initial reaction? Complete disbelief.

I think everyone understands how recruiters make money. This was not new information. So, was there really a need to publicly deliver such a patronising message to candidates who are already navigating one of the toughest markets we've seen in years?

The underlying tone suggested something far more revealing: candidates are treated as byproducts of the process: secondary, inconvenient, and an operational burden rather than an integral stakeholder.

If the goal was engagement, she definitely succeeded; more than sixty responses rolled in. A few recruiters echoed her view (which honestly makes me question how we still have a functioning industry), but the overwhelming majority were from candidates who were angry and exhausted. Their complaints were remarkably consistent:

"*A recruiter contacted me, said I was a perfect fit for a role, and then I never heard from them again.*"

This is not ignorance on their part. This is the emotional fallout of a dynamic we created.

All in all, not very clean soulish.

Aidan Murray's Post:

The next post in my feed could not have been more different.

It opened with a screenshot of an email from a candidate who had just accepted a role elsewhere. No placement or fee. Just a short message thanking Aidan for the support, honesty, and guidance he'd given throughout their conversations.

Aidan explained that a recruiter's value isn't defined solely by placements. He speaks to hundreds of people each year who are good at what they do, many of whom will never become a placement, at least not immediately. Those conversations are not written off as wasted time; they're treated as part of the market he operates in.

He described how those interactions often involve helping candidates make sense of where they sit, what's realistic, how hiring decisions actually get made, and what they may need to change or accept before a move makes sense. Sometimes that guidance leads to a role months or even years later. Sometimes it doesn't.

Either way, the relationship holds.

The email he shared demonstrated the outcome of that approach perfectly. No commercial gain, yet genuine trust. When that person needs a recruiter again, whether as a candidate or a client, there is no competition, the decision has already been made.

This isn't altruism. It's a strategy.

Aidan treats candidates as long-term market equity, not transactional outputs. He understands that candidate conversations compound. They resurface as referrals, warm re-engagements, future clients, and advocates who defend your reputation when the industry comes under fire.

That's why his results stack over time.

Where the first post framed candidates as a necessary inconvenience, this one showed something else entirely: candidates as stakeholders. People whose experience travels far beyond a single role.

Plenty of recruiters consistently work this way. The problem is that this mindset is still treated as optional, even indulgent, in an industry that has long believed candidates should be grateful for our attention.

They're not, and the ones who understand that are already pulling away.

So no, this isn't about becoming a career coach or running a free advice clinic. It's about recognising that reputation is built in the conversations that don't pay immediately, and destroyed in the ones we treat as disposable.

In short: be more Aidan.

At this point, it's tempting to lay the blame on everything but us.

We have no influence or control over what's happening in the market, the economic landscape, the shortage of jobs, the direction and pace of AI, or the apathy and desperation of candidates when their backs are against the wall.

If we can't do anything about the above, why are we still clinging to an attitude we could change tomorrow?

The one thing we *do* have complete control over is how we see candidates.

When we choose to let go of an ingrained mindset and start seeing candidates as an economic engine rather than an inconvenience, everything starts to change.

This choice shapes trust: elevates our reputation, and dictates whether candidates engage with us as partners or treat us as another obstacle to overcome.

Once you accept that, the fixes show up in very ordinary places: how we reject, how we follow up, and how that first conversation actually sounds.

There are two recurring issues in the candidate experience that do more damage to our reputation than anything else, and both are entirely within our control to fix.

The first is application overload, and what happens when candidates hear nothing back. The second is what happens when *we* initiate contact, raise expectations, and then disappear.

Application Overload

In a market like this, it's simply not possible to read every CV properly, let alone speak to everyone who applies. Many won't be relevant. Many will be speculative. Many will be driven by panic rather than fit.

From the candidate's side, that's understandable. When jobs feel scarce and rejection feels constant, volume becomes a survival tactic. Apply widely, quickly, and hope something lands.

From the recruiter's side, it's overwhelming. When most applications don't meet the brief, disengagement starts to creep in. We are not being callous, but there's only so much time, energy, and headspace to go around. Silence starts to feel like the only way to cope.

This is where the dynamic turns toxic. Candidates feel ignored and dismissed. We feel buried. The more candidates apply indiscriminately, the less recruiters respond. The less we respond, the more candidates panic and apply to everything. It feeds itself.

At its worst, silence becomes a quiet form of punishment. A way of signalling, consciously or not, that if someone applies for the wrong role, they shouldn't expect a response. A bit like hoping silence will give a dodgy ex the hint.

This isn't a new phenomenon.

After the global financial crash in 2008, jobs fell off a cliff and redundancies were prolific. Unemployment rose sharply, from a baseline of 5% to 8% by 2011, hitting those just entering the workplace the hardest.

Applications flooded in, phone lines lit up, and suddenly we were dealing with volumes we couldn't physically manage. Candidates were chasing anything that looked like a way back into work.

Back then, just as now, the industry needed a way to cope.

Most agencies leaned harder on rejection templates, when time allowed. Many leaned on silence instead. I went in a different direction.

To address application overload without resorting to silence, I stopped using the standard rejection template altogether.

I replaced it with what I call the "Missed Info Rejection Email."

TO: Candidate@me.com

SUBJECT: Application Update:

Thank you for the time you put into your application for **[Job Title/Ref]**.

I'll be honest: I'm struggling to see a clear link between your experience and the specific outcomes this position requires.

However, we've been overwhelmed with applications lately, and I'm only human. It is not beyond the realms of possibility that I may have missed something essential or misread a key part of your background while working through the volume.

If you believe there is specific information I've missed that relates to this role, you are very welcome to reply with the subject line:
[Missed Info – Job Ref].

If you can highlight the key areas you'd like me to reconsider, I will personally review them.

If I don't hear from you, I genuinely wish you the very best of luck with your search.

It's something I've used ever since, regardless of how the market was swinging. On paper, this may feel risky. It requires acknowledging that you are human, that you can overlook things, and that not every decision is perfect.

In a hiring process increasingly dominated by keywords, bots, and algorithms, that admission strengthens your authority, not weakens it. When a human enters a process that often feels mechanical and opaque to candidates, it cuts through.

A common concern is that this will invite an avalanche of follow-up emails or calls. In practice, the opposite happens. Using a right of reply makes the desk more efficient, not less. Here's why:

It closes the loop

The number one reason candidates spam recruiters with "Any update?" or "Why was I rejected?" is a lack of closure. By stating exactly why you are hesitant, the lack of a clear link, you provide that closure. Most candidates who know they are a "stretch" will see your honesty, realise they can't bridge the gap, and quietly move on.

It encourages candidate self-selection
When you ask for a specific subject line and "specific information I've missed," you are raising the bar.

This requires the candidate to do homework.

Only the high-intent candidates who feel genuinely overlooked will put in the effort to reply. The "spam" applications drop off because they have nothing to provide.

It turns "search" into "quality control."
We all know the "Recruiter Fatigue" that sets in after 500 CVs. We do miss things. Instead of spending your time defending your decisions against angry emails or calls, you are outsourcing the "double-check" to the candidate.

The unintended benefit of this approach is that it doesn't just improve the candidate experience; it improves the desk.

You spend less time chasing, defending, and explaining decisions. You stop having circular conversations with candidates who were never right in the first place. The only replies you receive are from people who can articulate relevance, and those are precisely the conversations worth having.

It sends a very subtle message to candidates that it's only worth applying for jobs they are suited to, and that their CV demonstrates that relevance.

It narrows your focus to the candidates that matter, surfaces people who would otherwise be missed, and reduces the background noise that drains time and energy.

It also does something far more valuable: it changes how candidates perceive us and elevates our personal brands.

Try it. You'll see very quickly the difference it will make to your sanity.

You can thank me later.

The Second Candidate Grievance

A major gripe candidates have with recruiters is this one, and it's entirely of our own making.

We approach them, call them out of the blue, tell them their CV looks brilliant, say they're an ideal match, sometimes even use the words "perfect fit," take a few details, build a bit of momentum, and then say we'll send their CV over to the client.

Then we ghost them.

The candidate, who didn't even apply in the first place, is left scratching their head. They follow up, chase. Eventually, they stop expecting anything at all.

I could dress this up and call it "poor process" or a "communication breakdown," but from the outside, it looks like we blew smoke up their backsides and left them hanging out to dry. That's the part candidates remember.

Now, before anyone reaches for the defensive playbook, I would like to be very clear about something: most recruiters are not deliberately ghosting candidates. We're not being malicious.

What's usually happening is far more mundane.

We simply forget. It's very difficult to keep track of everyone we call, especially if the conversation doesn't lead to anything concrete. Our job is to "find the one," which means kissing a lot of frogs, right? These poor souls are just collateral damage.

We tell them nice, ego-boosting things because we think that will get engagement and "buy-in," making it sting even more when they never hear from us again.

We shy away from voicing our doubts and concerns and telling them they are not a fit. We don't want to burst their bubble or be confrontational, so silence becomes the path of least resistance and justification.

The job goes quiet or gets put on hold, but we forget who we've spoken to already and neglect to inform them.

This becomes normalised behaviour that just gets folded into the daily routine. The reality of this is that we are quietly hammering another nail into our reputation by treating people as disposable.

Not all recruiters do this, but enough for it to be "a thing" when it doesn't need to be a thing at all.

The Following 5-Point Fix Is Probably the Easiest in the Entire Book

When We Start the Conversation, We Own the Outcome

#1 Stop promising anything on a first call.
If you're calling around to get your numbers up, or casually saying you'll send a CV to the client just to keep the conversation flowing, stop. Nothing good comes from that, ever. False momentum still creates false hope.

#2 Tell them when they're not quite right.
If you're on the call and something doesn't sit properly, say so. There is no need to be patronising or defensive, just honest. Closing the loop in real time builds far more trust than vague encouragement followed by silence.

If there is something there, don't force it. If you rush it on the first call, you will fail to build any sort of relationship. Book a separate alignment call. You are never going to uncover everything you need on a first reach-out anyway. Fastest finger first has had its moment.

#3 Follow up immediately with intent.
Send a confirmation email straight after that first call, setting out exactly what the next conversation is for:

Checking alignment with their career goals
What the client is actually trying to solve
Making sure neither of you is wasting your time

This reframes the process as mutual decision-making rather than a one-sided audition.

#4 Do the alignment call properly.
Video or voice, at least 30 minutes. Not squeezed between calls or half-listened to.

In the next chapter, we will look at live candidate calls that demonstrate this process. We'll walk through this exact scenario step by step, so you can see how it plays out in practice rather than theory.

#5 Commit to an update, even if there isn't one.
Set a reminder to update them within five working days. Call or email, either is fine. Tell them what you did, what happened, and if it's not going anywhere.

Honesty beats silence, hands down. It's about stopping ourselves from creating the very distrust we keep whinging about.

This is about building a desk that isn't fighting you every day.

When candidates know where they stand, they stop clogging up your inbox and headspace. This approach reduces noise.

You build a reusable pipeline. Candidates you close the loop with come back, refer others, and resurface when the timing is right. That's future commercial value you didn't have to source.

You stop burning bridges you didn't know you were standing on. Today's "nearly right" candidate is tomorrow's client, tomorrow's hiring manager, and a future referral source. Ghost them once, and you don't just lose them, you lose their memory of you. Reputation compounds, good and bad.

Your conversations get sharper, faster. When you stop promising CV submissions on first calls, your conversations become more intentional, your alignment calls get better, and your qualification improves. You waste less time convincing and more time aligning. That's desk efficiency, not ethics.

You become the recruiter people actually respond to. In a market full of AI messages, vague outreach and empty enthusiasm, being transparent, honest, and consistent is now a differentiator. Candidates reply to recruiters they trust. Clients trust recruiters who show respect for candidates because this has a knock-on effect in the shortlists you send, how the candidate shows up on their first day, and how they pan out whilst in the job.

That's the loop that feeds fees.

Closing the Loop: Mindset Before Method

The overriding objective of this book, and this chapter in particular, has been to examine how we elevate our industry's reputation.

The two very practical fixes that are entirely within our control are how we respond to applications and how we handle our initial candidate conversations. Both are simple. Neither requires more time, new software, or additional process.

They help, but on their own, they are not enough. Without embedding the three core principles into those first candidate interactions, we will continue to struggle to build trust, and without trust, everything else remains fragile.

Mindset

Repairing our reputation is no longer optional. It is critical to the survival of our industry. The starting point isn't process or technology, but how we see and treat candidates.

At the beginning of this chapter, we examined how many of us are still viewing candidates through an outdated lens. A mindset that no longer serves us, the market, or the outcomes we want.

When we change how we show up for candidates, how we handle those first interactions, and how consistently we apply that standard to everyone, everything else begins to shift.

When candidates sense that we are working towards their agenda rather than our own, trust starts to build. Once trust is in play, results compound.

If we are serious about elevating our reputation, there is one behaviour we must let go of completely.

We must stop screening candidates.

Screening: The Habit That Gives Us Away

I've spent over a quarter of a century in this industry, and I've never quite understood this screening malarkey.

We don't screen clients.
We don't screen jobs.
We explore, we evaluate, we qualify.

But candidates? We screen. Like airport security or customs control, like we are trying to catch them out.

I know it may sound like semantics, but the language alone tells the story. Screening implies suspicion. It assumes there is something wrong to be uncovered before trust is earned. It places us in a position of authority and the candidate in a position of defence.

When the label "screen" sits in our head, consciously or not, we prime ourselves to extract information and interrogate:

"What are your salary expectations?"
"Why did you leave?"
"WHERE WERE YOU ON THE NIGHT OF THE FIFTEENTH?"
"What have you achieved?"

When we choose exploration instead, we sit alongside the candidate. We create the right environment for honesty. Problems surface earlier. Misalignment reveals itself before it becomes expensive. Fallout, backtracking, and unpleasant surprises are reduced dramatically.

Screening creates short-term reassurance. Exploration creates long-term stability. If we want better answers, alignment, and outcomes, we must stop creating environments where honesty feels risky.

So let's ditch the spotlight and invite them to sit at the table.

Stop screening and start exploring.
Stop vetting and start validating.

Let's stop looking for red flags and start noticing human ones.

Call it a qualifying call, a discovery call, an initial call, call it whatever you want. Just eradicate the word screen.

In the next chapter, we will review the live calls and demonstrate the three core principles in action.

You'll see how relationships are established from the very first interaction, how the questions we ask turn candidate conversations from interrogation to collaboration, and how a "them-first" mindset underpins it all.

This is what partnership and alignment looks like in practice.

The Initial Candidate calls next. Bring something steady. No sugar spike. This is about composure.

Candidate Armageddon Rap-Up
All About the Rep

Inbox full of "any update?" crap,
Five calls missed, still chasing Jack,
CV reads fine, reality's slack,
But yeah, let's screen 'em like a customs hack.

Candidates clock how you make 'em feel,
Not the job, not the pitch, but the deal,
Safe hands turn honesty real,
Fear-led questions get half-truths sealed.

This ain't fluffy, this is currency,
Trust gets spent, saved, earned currently,
Reputational rot don't show day one,
But it kills your desk when the damage is done.

Some call it luck, some understandin',
Long game trust, that's Aidan's branding,
It's critical, this is our survival,
Get ready now for a **Clean Soul** revival.

Chapter 10

The Initial Candidate Call

(Formerly Known as the Screen)

Candidates aren't a formality in the process; they are the process. They're the constant, no matter which way the market swings: feast, famine, candidate-short, job-short, recession, boom, or whatever fresh chaos LinkedIn is panicking about this week.

When you stop pushing, prodding, persuading, and performing, something magical happens. Your desk stops feeling like a battlefield and starts feeling... dare we say... enjoyable.

Whilst all candidates are unique, they share one common denominator: all career decisions are driven by emotion, not logic.

You can draw a line down the centre of a page until the biro runs dry, line up the pros and list the cons, and they'll still go with whatever hits them square in the chest. They will back all emotion-based decisions with logic, but it never leads or works in reverse.

So instead of trying to convince candidates, the Clean Soul way is to create a safe environment where they can actually think. When you tap into their motivations, fears, frustrations, hopes, and internal drivers without steering, shaping, or manipulating, you build trust very quickly.

Treat candidates like the living, thinking, feeling core of the journey and watch how they become the evangelical engine that drives your reputation.

This is how you reduce ghosting, prevent counteroffers, and stop dropouts before they happen.

It all starts on the very first call.

Now… before we get into the conversation itself, let's look at the usual culprits: the questions that shut candidates down long before they've had the chance to trust you.

Questions to Avoid

AVOID: What's your current situation?
REPLACE: What's happening for you at work, if anything, that's made you open to this conversation?

AVOID: Why did you leave your current/last role?
REPLACE: What was happening just before you decided to move on?

AVOID: What sort of role are you looking for?
REPLACE: What needs to be different between your current role and your next one?

AVOID: What are your salary expectations?
REPLACE: What package would you need for a move to make sense?

AVOID: Would you be able to work 100% on-site?
REPLACE: What would you be giving up to be on-site full-time?

The Candidate Conversation

We have won over Nordalyn as a prospect (Chapter 6, Scenario 3). They have given us a Technical Sales Engineer role to work on (Chapter 7), and now we are looking at delivery, the candidate side.

It's been a week since I last spoke to Darren, and I have been in full-throttle search mode. There has been a decent response to the ads I put out, and I have had conversations with several applicants, but although good, they didn't quite meet the criteria for the role.

We all know that rocking horse sh*t isn't queuing up out the back, so I've also been doing my outreach to see if relevant people in the industry would be open to a conversation.

But let's pause for a second, because outreach today has become a crime scene.

It's often viewed as an admin task you can dump onto an AI bot. As a result, candidates are getting spammed with generic, lifeless messages that make "hope you're well" feel like a personal attack.

Parasites are preying on desperate job seekers, draining their bank balances and dragging the recruitment industry's reputation through the mud. LinkedIn isn't policing it nearly enough; anyone with a laptop and a pulse can pretend to be a recruiter. So, candidates are understandably anxious, suspicious, and actually scared to respond to outreach.

So, if you are outreaching on LinkedIn... own it. Make it human, safe, and obviously not written by a spammy cockroach.

Here is an example of how I do mine. This approach gets me around an 82% response rate. By the way, it's not my original; a recruiter once sent me something similar and it stopped me in my tracks...

Subject: Bit of a long shot...

I appreciate that recruiter outreach must drive you around the bend, and I am not surprised, given your skills and experience.

However, I could not resist letting you know about a role I am working on for a [brief role details -e.g., senior X role within Y sector, focused on ZI]. I've attached a short overview for context.

I'm not assuming this will be relevant to you, or even that you are looking to make a move, but it would be great if you could let me know.

If it is of interest, I would be happy to share more details and answer any questions (full transparency and no commitment on your part)

If the timing is off, or the role isn't right: no problem, but I would love the chance to connect, as it's always great to have people of your calibre in my network.

Please feel free to look at my profile to be satisfied that I'm not a bot or worse, a scammer.

This is how I came to be having a conversation with Freja, the candidate you're about to meet.

I sent her the example InMail after spotting her profile. I didn't expect a reply; her background was a bit too on-the-nose: 13 years of selling technical equipment into the food industry. Six years of work history in Denmark and the last seven in the UK, working for a highly respected organisation. She also has an engineering qualification. Recruiters like me probably hound her every week, but to my surprise, she responded the same day and we set up a time to chat.

I am deliberately showcasing this candidate, as it is easy to get carried away on a positive wave when we come across someone who ticks all the boxes. There is a reluctance to ask the questions that pose a risk of getting answers we may not want to hear.

This isn't a one-shot wonder of a conversation. What you're about to see is a two-stage Clean Soul process, because candidates deserve more than a rush-job interrogation disguised as "screening."

Call One – Exploration (the call you're about to read):

Here, my job was simple: help Freja explore her current situation, her motivations, her frustrations, and her vision of an ideal next step, without pushing her toward anything. Most candidate calls end here. If they do, they should end with the candidate feeling respected, clearer, and genuinely better off for having spoken with you.

Call Two – Exploring Value, Evaluation & Expectations (the next day on video):

When a candidate chooses to continue the journey, that's when we go deeper.

This second call is where we explore her track record, her achievements, her value to a role like this, and then, together, we walk through the Evaluation and Expectations stages of the Triple E Process.

And trust me, once you see how much she brings to that space, you'll understand why Part Two becomes not just appropriate... but inevitable.

Call One

What you're about to see is part one of our conversation, where I want to establish if there is any interest. I aim to build trust, whether she moves forward or not. Most candidate calls will end at this stage.

So, as you read, keep an eye on four things:

The mindset I'm working from
The relationship and trust I am cultivating throughout the call
The questions I ask, and just as importantly, don't
How I'm respecting her agenda, not trying to bend it around mine

We join the call just as Freja picks up. She sounds warm, curious, and possibly half-expecting to be disappointed...

Me: Hi Freja, thank you for responding to my message. I was hoping you would. What prompted you to come back so quickly?

Freja: I'm approached by recruiters all the time, but yours stood out. The role looks intriguing and seems to match my experience, so I'm curious to learn more.

Me: Looking at your profile, it's no surprise that you attract lots of interest. Your experience in the food sector is precisely what my client is looking for. I cannot wait to tell you more about the role at Nordalyn, but would you be comfortable if I asked...

(Interrupts me)

Commentary:
Notice something here? I mention the company name early, before

she even asks. Why? Because trust starts with transparency. I'm not playing the "I've got an amazing role at a secret company" game. That just raises suspicion and makes you sound like you're either bluffing or holding something back.

Freja: Nordalyn? But they're based in Denmark, right? I didn't think they were in the food industry.

Me: They have just started in the food industry. They've developed a predictive maintenance system, PMH. It's already very successful in other countries, and they're now building a UK team to launch it here.

Freja: Oh my god, the PMH system. Everybody is talking about this. It's causing quite a stir in my circles.

Me: Oh, you've heard of it?

Freja: Yes, but only from my customers and what I have read about it. I had no idea Nordalyn was behind it. I know the company quite well, as I'm Danish, but I didn't connect the dots. You've got my attention now.

Me: I'm happy to hear that. From all accounts, the product is practically selling itself. Looking at your profile, you've been at Pureline for around seven years now. What types of products are you selling there?

Freja: Primarily, I work with vision monitoring systems for high-compliance food and pharma sites. The backbone of my work, though, is with chilled food producers. I don't have experience with maintenance systems, but I understand the challenges that a food production plant faces due to downtime.

Me: That sounds quite technical. What's happening with your current role at the moment that has got you peeking over the fence?

Freja: Well, I'm not actively looking. To be honest, I love the company, but I'm worried that they aren't innovating with their products at all. There is so much more they could be developing in terms of being faster and more intuitive. As the market leader in this field, they seem to be getting quite complacent, which is a shame. Our competition isn't standing still.

Commentary:
Here's where the exploration begins. My question might sound light: "What's got you peeking over the fence?" but don't be fooled. It's deliberately soft, open, and disarming. I'm not asking why she wants to leave. That's too binary. Instead, I'm inviting her to reflect on her current landscape and hint at what might be missing. And bingo, look at what she gives me. She's not disengaged or bitter. She's loyal. She still loves the company, but there's a slow-burning frustration here: a lack of innovation, a creeping sense that her company's falling behind while the competition sharpens their knives. This is where I start mentally building the gap. I'm listening for three things: her current situation, what's caused the shift, and what ideal looks like. That's the heart of this stage, gap analysis. What's the distance between where she is and where she wants to be? More importantly, what's stopping her from closing that gap herself?

Me: Oh no, that sounds like it could have an impact on your career. How have you tried to address this with them?

Freja: I've constantly tried, even offered to help with strategy, but nothing's changed. I'm beginning to think I care more about progress than they do.

Me: How long has this been this way?

Freja: It must be about 12 months. I thought things might change. Don't get me wrong; if they had made some progress in developing the products, I wouldn't hesitate to stay, but as things stand, I feel I need to look at alternatives.

Me: That's sad, because you sound very loyal and committed to them. What was it that made you join them in the first place?

Freja: Well, I chose them, not the other way around. I targeted them, even though they did not have a job going at the time. I had just moved to the UK after getting married, and I researched the company. I then called them up and told them what I could do for them, given my previous experience in Denmark. I knew they were looking to expand their chilled food division, and I was confident I could help them achieve that. They created a role for me but took a significant risk by taking me on.

Me: Risky, how?

Freja: I had no prior experience with UK clients, so I had to build my customer base from scratch. Don't get me wrong, I proved my value in my first year and have delivered what they want ever since. They were very supportive and provided me with extensive training. I will always be grateful that they took a chance on me.

Me: I know that feeling. That sense of loyalty can really stick, even when things no longer work. What would a new job look like that is different from what you have now?

Commentary:
This next bit is where many recruiters start seeing pound signs. She's engaged, enthusiastic, and clearly frustrated with her current company. On the surface, she might look like a walking fee, but if you're paying attention, there's something deeper going on. Freja didn't just land her current job; she built it. She chose the company, pitched herself, and convinced them to create a role. Her story is intricately tied to that job. So yes, she may be frustrated now, but that kind of emotional investment doesn't just vanish, it sticks. This is where the temptation to fast-track things kicks in. But pushing forward here would be like decorating a house you haven't checked for dry rot. The counteroffer risk isn't just financial, it's emotional, so I'm going to slow it down. Unless we've explored how deeply her roots go, we've no idea how likely she is to move or snap back when the pressure's on.

Freja: In truth, it would have to offer pioneering products for the food sector, the same type of role, with the same customers, and I'd also like to see some proper opportunities for career growth.

I'm currently on a salary of £70k plus an annual bonus, and I wouldn't want to go below that. Additionally, I'd like to explore more niches within the food sector.

Me: Okay, that's great. So, let me make sure I have this right. You are not actively searching for a new role. However, you're a bit miffed that Pureline isn't developing its current products, which is getting you worried about the competition moving in on your customers. You have approached them about this, but they keep fobbing you off, so you feel your best chance would be to explore new opportunities. You would like a similar job to what you already have, but one that involves selling a stronger product and exploring new niche sectors. You don't want to compromise on the package you are already on, either. Is there anything else?

Freja: That's right, I can't think of anything else at the moment. Do you think Nordalyn would be interested in looking at me?

Me: I'm sure they would. Your profile aligns well with the job brief. Having felt this way for the past year, what has stopped you from actively reaching out to the market or your competition until now?

Freja: Ah, can I be frank with you here? About eight months ago, I was approached by our main competitor, and they offered me a job with a significant salary increase. I was very excited about the opportunity and wanted to accept. However, I went to hand in my notice, and Pureline was horrified. It really took them by surprise, so they offered me even more money, which I rightly or wrongly accepted. I hope that won't put you off helping me.

Commentary:
And here it is, she drops the "C-word," and not just any counteroffer, one that she accepted. I'll be honest, this caught me off guard. I'm *not judging her, far from it. It's because this is one of those make-or-break signals. A counteroffer in someone's history is like a fault line under the surface. It tells you the story isn't simple, and if you don't dig deeper, you're walking straight into a rerun. But it's not just the content of what she said, it's how she said it. There was zero polish, spin, or trying to downplay it. She told me straight. That's*

rare. In a world where candidates often feel they have to "manage" recruiters, this kind of raw honesty tells me she trusts me enough not to hold it against her. So I *don't jump to conclusions. I don't switch gears and start risk-managing her. I stay with her. Keep listening. Because yes, it's a red flag. But it's also a green light for a much more honest conversation.*

Me: Not at all. Thank you for being so open with me. I can't blame Pureline for doing that. How do you think they will respond if you were to give your notice for a second time?

Freja: I think they will try to keep me, but this time it's different. I wouldn't accept it.

Me: You sound pretty confident about that.

Freja: Absolutely. I made the mistake of having my head turned before. I was so stupid that I told them who my customers were during the interview. They have just poached one of them from me, whose contract had expired, and there will be more in the future, especially as Pureline is not making the necessary changes to remain competitive. If I leave this time, I certainly won't be going to a competitor, and Pureline has had ample time to resolve this issue. Money isn't the issue, so it doesn't matter what they throw at me.

Me: I can see that you would need to be very strategic with your next career move and ensure that the company isn't competing with them. What would you need to know about the role at Nordalyn to be satisfied that it is worth considering?

Closing Summary

Following this, we spent some time going through the role. I didn't "oversell" the job; instead, I discussed what they were looking to achieve, the company's structure, and we chatted more about the PMH system. She knew more about it than I did. But the real substance, her achievements, her story, and how I can position her, will still need to be unpacked. So we agreed to pick things up properly via Teams the next day. She'd send over her CV after the call. I'd send her the job spec and spend time looking at how we might align her profile with what the client actually needs, not just what the job ad says.

Call Two: The Alignment Call

Freja's CV is impressive and would guarantee her an interview at Nordalyn without any input from me. Although sending it to me and agreeing to a video call suggests she is interested, I am not assuming anything. She could change her mind at any time. She has complete control over her decisions and the way she responds to my questions. All I have control over is the process. There is no such thing as "controlling the candidate". There never was.

The primary objective of this stage is to understand how Freja will add value to this particular role and how it will benefit her. She has already been briefed on the information I will need, and I always find it best to discuss this on a separate call from the initial one. This way, they are more focused. Determining their value can be a challenging process. Some candidates struggle to articulate this and go off on deflective tangents, beat around the bush, and ultimately fail to provide you with anything tangible. This is where framing the right questions, whilst maintaining the right environment for them to answer honestly, comes into its own.

Me: Hi Freja, it's great to meet you. Thanks for sending me your CV. It's helpful to see the full context of your work history. I know we only spoke yesterday, and having had a chance to sleep on it, has anything shifted for you overnight?

Commentary:
This early check-in shows her I'm not assuming enthusiasm sticks. It gives her permission to voice doubts without losing face.

Freja: And it's lovely to meet you too. I've been very excited about this since yesterday. If anything, I'm more curious now. I've taken a thorough look at their website and spoken to someone I know who has recently mentioned their systems. It's still early days, but it's got some great, unique selling points.

Me: Yes, it has indeed. From what I know, the product can save a significant amount of money on downtime. The reason I was keen to take it to this stage is so I can position you in the best possible way to Nordalyn, if you are still happy to be put forward, that is. I'm keen to understand what your proudest moments have been, including the commercials, and what makes you a standout candidate. Is that something you are comfortable with?

Freja: Absolutely, I am. Ask me anything.

Me: Brilliant. When we spoke yesterday, you mentioned that you had targeted Pureline to secure a job. I was so impressed with your resilience; it must have been daunting making a fresh start in a new country. How did you go about building your UK customer base from scratch?

Freja: It was. I had no contacts and no live opportunities. So, I researched the chilled food producers growing the fastest, mapped their factory locations, and then spent a month visiting sites and asking questions. I also attended sector events where their engineering teams would show up. I didn't even sell to them; I just asked what wasn't working and took notes.

Commentary:
Freja's not describing luck; she's describing method. This is great for positioning her later, but more importantly, it reminds her she built her UK career from scratch.

Me: That sounds like a very proactive and consultative approach.

Freja: (laughs) I like to think so. I listen before I sell. I think that's why Pureline gave me a shot.

Me: Was there ever a moment in your role when you thought, "Yes, this is why they hired me"? A moment that felt like yours?

Freja: Hmm... I think that when I brought in two new clients in my first year, Silverstone Produce and Rivendale Ready Meals. Both were long-term users of a competitor. However, I brought them over by offering a phased system upgrade that addressed their hygiene audit weaknesses without disrupting production. That was huge. We weren't even on their radar before.

Me: So, in your first year here, you didn't just win new clients, you converted from long-term competitors by solving compliance gaps others had overlooked. That's not just about sales; it's about repositioning the value Pureline brings.

Freja: I'd like to think it was my approach. I did a full site audit for them first and just walked them through what their systems were missing. One of them came back three months later and said, "Nobody's explained it to us like that before."

Commentary:
I don't jump straight into the commercials. I linger on the human aspect, specifically what she believes led them to switch, so she views her own approach as the key differentiator.

Me: I love that. I noticed in your CV that you hit 121% of target last year. What was your target?

Freja: It was £2.5 million, and I did just over three. This year, it's £2.8 million, and I'm already at £2.3 with some good stuff in the pipeline, so I'm all set to hit that.

Commentary:
This now leads me to ask Freja several standard questions about the length of her sales cycle, average value of order, etc. Rather than listing each one of these in the script, I will simply summarise what she has told me. Her answers demonstrated ownership, not just participation. I'm building a story I can share with Nordalyn, but more importantly, she's seeing herself in the story as well.

Me: Wow, that's very impressive. Can I just make sure I have written everything down correctly? Apart from being on track to deliver against a £2.8 million target this year, your average sales cycle length ranges from 6 to 12 months. Your typical order value is around £150k, but you also have several at £250k. Out of the four salespeople at Pureline, you have consistently delivered the most revenue and profit year after year. You cover all of the UK and Northern Ireland. Have I missed anything out?

Freja: Yes, you've got everything right. You're either an excellent listener or a great note taker.

Me: Bit of both, I think. What has really stood out for me, though, is that you have consistently been Pureline's top salesperson. What is it that you do that's different from the others there?

Freja: I just don't treat it like a sales pitch. First and foremost, I like to think of myself as a problem solver, and this is where my engineering mindset comes into play. I want my customers to know I can fix their issues. They come to me first to sort out problems, even before discussing them with their ops teams. One of my customers recently told me I was like a bloodhound because I wouldn't give up until I had resolved something.

Commentary:
A playful label like that is priceless. Clients remember metaphors. My job is to tuck it away for later and reflect it back to Nordalyn.

Me: You sound really passionate about your customers. I can see why Pureline is very lucky to have you. What sort of people would you typically deal with in the sales process?

Freja: It's multi-layered. The QA has a good understanding of the compliance issues they are facing and how these can impact the business, which could be catastrophic. Still, it's also essential to have the Engineering Managers, finance, and right up to the director level. Decisions of this nature are never down to just one person, so I have to network throughout the business.

Me: It sounds like you have to navigate around many different demands. How do you manage and align all those stakeholders?

Freja: I think it's the bit I enjoy the most. Most of the time, I'm on the shop floor, but I'm just as comfortable sitting in a boardroom. I treat them all with the same level of respect.

Me: I know where you are coming from. I like to operate in the same way. I noticed on your CV that you have a 97% conversion rate on your tenders. That's really impressive. What involvement do you have in that?

Freja: 100% involvement. I prefer to compile my own testimonials of similar previous work, handle the pricing, and maintain control, as this approach increases the win rate and builds more trust with potential clients. I handle all pre-sales work, conduct site audits, provide system training, and even project-manage installations.

Me: So, you're not only opening doors, but you're also closing them with near certainty, and you're staying accountable from first audit to final install. That gives me a full-cycle story to tell Nordalyn: consistency, control, and trust. Does Pureline offer you any support with this?

Freja: Yes, they do, and they support when I need it, but I'm a bit of a control freak, so I prefer to do this myself.

Me: How do you manage that type of workload?

Freja: It takes some juggling, but it's worth it. It gives me complete control over how the solution is positioned, and it means my clients only ever deal with me. They love that. There are no Chinese whispers, no confusion, just one accountable point of contact. That's probably my biggest differentiator.

Me: And it clearly shows in your figures. After the equipment has been implemented, what sort of difference has it made to the customer?

Freja: That's a good question. One of the recurring pieces of feedback I receive, especially from QA, is that the systems give them breathing space. Previously, they were constantly firefighting. Now, with the monitoring dashboards and alerts we've implemented, they can identify issues early and address them proactively. From an engineering perspective, it's usually about reducing downtime. One Engineering Manager told me that just one of the modules we installed saved them nearly four hours of unplanned stoppage per month. Doesn't sound like much, but in chilled food production, that's massive; it's lost revenue, wasted product, and usually a migraine for everyone. I think what changes most is the level of stress. One client said, "It's the first time in years we've gone a quarter without a compliance panic." That meant a lot.

Me: Freja, thank you. You've given me a clear picture of what you can bring, and I can already see how much value you could add to Nordalyn. At the same time, you've been with Pureline for seven years and built something solid. Before either of us gets carried away, it's just as essential to make sure this move would be right for you. Would you be comfortable if I asked you a few more questions with that in mind?

Commentary:
She's sharp. Every answer is clean, and the numbers back her up. On paper, she's the one you dream of finding. But I've been around the block a few times to know that when someone looks this flawless, there's usually something lurking and ready to pounce underneath. This stage shows me the strengths. The next stage will tell me whether those strengths survive the messy middle. For now, I'll hold the thought: brilliant, but maybe a touch too good to be true. Trust me when I say, the restraint is almost physical.

Evaluation: Risk, Resistance, and Readiness

If the last part of this conversation was about value, this one is about weight. This is where the invisible obstacles begin to surface. Not objections exactly, but rather emotional gravity, things that pull a candidate back when logic suggests moving forward. We're going to examine the impact of staying, the cost of leaving, and the emotional undercurrent that most recruiters often overlook. There'll be no objections to handle, just questions to explore. What's really at stake if she makes the move, and what's holding her where she is?

Me: If this move goes ahead, what do you think might start to shift or change for you and those around you?

Commentary:
I am trying to understand how a move might affect others in her life, as family is often the deal-breaker when considering an offer. I know I am getting ahead of myself, as she hasn't been interviewed yet, but this is stuff she needs to start thinking about and preparing herself for.

Freja: Hmm... I think the first shift would be in my mindset. Right now, I'm cruising a bit, managing accounts, doing well, but not really stretching myself. A new role like this would certainly shake that up. I'd be back in growth mode again, which I miss. At home, my husband's work is stable, and his family is close by, which really helps, as we have a three-year-old daughter. I'm aware that change doesn't just affect me. Even small things, such as adjusting nursery times or my need to travel more, might impact her routine. I wouldn't want to take on something I couldn't fully commit to.

Me: That makes complete sense, and it's refreshing to hear someone think not just about what they can do, but also about what they can give to a new role without compromise. What would need to be in place for you to feel confident that you could make that transition smoothly, both personally and professionally?

Freja: I think clarity would be helpful. Understanding the support the company provides to its sales team, the onboarding process, and travel management would be beneficial. I'm not afraid of hard work; I never have been. However, I'm protective of where my energy is directed these days. May I ask how realistic you think Nordalyn's expectations are, based on what you know of the role so far? Are they open to someone like me stepping in and shaking things up a bit, or are they looking for someone just to keep things ticking along?

Me: That's a cracking question, and exactly the kind of edge I hoped you'd bring. They are looking for a shaker. There is no territory, so you would be expected to evolve and shape the division for this product. They're scaling up, not coasting, but I'll be digging into that further before your CV goes across, because they must be ready for the kind of impact you bring.

Freja: Perfect, because I'm not in the market for babysitting a pipeline. If I make a move, it's because I see potential for both of us.

Commentary:
I am dreading asking her this next question, because I know ultimately this would be her reason for staying at her current job. She has been carried away with the excitement of this role, but I now need to get her to look at her reality and what she potentially will have to deal with.

Me: I'm glad you're seeing things that way. I got the impression they were a family-friendly company when I met with them. Earlier, you spoke about how you go above and beyond for your clients, how much they trust you, and how you seem equally passionate about them; it's very rare to hear that these days. If you were to leave Pureline, how will this impact your customers?

Freja: (Silence. Then a strange expression crosses her face.) That's... not something I've thought about. I mean, I know they rely on me; I've built many of those accounts from scratch. I suppose... I'd be leaving them mid-journey, wouldn't I? Some of those projects are still in motion, and even if someone else takes over, it wouldn't be the same. (Quiet pause.) But then again, if I stayed just because of them, I'd probably end up resenting it. That's not fair to anyone, either. (Another pause.) Perhaps there's a way I can still support them, even if I've moved on. Not officially, but... I don't know. That's something I'd have to think through.

Commentary:
That was tough going for her. I'm not looking to address her concerns; she will need to figure that out on her own. However, once she recognises that it will impact her, then she will automatically

start figuring out how to fix it.

Me: That's a lot to take in, and it's clear how much you care about the people you work with. Whether you stay or go, only you can determine what feels right. My role here is simply to ensure you have everything you need to weigh all the options properly.

Freja: Thank you, I appreciate it, but no more scary questions, please.

Me: No promises... but I'll tread gently. If you were to decide to stay at Pureline, how do you envision that impacting your career over the next year or two?

Freja: (Sighs.) Honestly, I think I'd continue doing what I'm doing: keeping clients happy, hitting targets, and staying reliable, but I can already feel it. Not burnout, exactly... more like I'm on autopilot. I know the rhythm, I know the objections, I know which clients will say yes before I even ask. It's steady, but it's no longer exciting, and I don't think they see me as someone to invest in beyond what I already deliver. (Brief pause.) The truth is, I don't want to be the person who stayed because it was easy. That's not why I joined them in the first place.

Me: Thanks for being so open with me, Freja. It feels like we've covered a lot of ground just now, not just about the role itself, but about what it actually means to you. I know this is about timing, energy, and ensuring you have enough of yourself left at the end of the day for your little one. Leaving behind clients you've nurtured and built trust with, is not a small thing. You're not looking to walk away from your values; you're looking for a way forward that honours them. As for staying put, you've been honest about what that might look like too. Reliable and safe, but perhaps not the stretch you're ready for. Does that sound about right?

Closing Commentary:
That was heavy. She's not skirting the questions; she's actually grappling with them, and that's what I needed: not interview polish, but real reflection. Her CV still shines, but now I see the weight

underneath: family, loyalty, the pull of the familiar. None of this makes her weaker; it makes the decision real. My job isn't to tidy it up or give her answers. It's simply to let her hear herself, and she's starting to do precisely that.

Expectations:

I am going to take a different tack with this stage. I can sense that Freja is dying to ask me some questions. This is quite normal with candidates and has the benefit of covering what's important to them. So, this next bit, she's in the driving seat, steering the conversation, raising any concerns and setting the pace.

Me: I'm very aware that I have asked you lots of questions so far, and I get the feeling that you are dying to ask me some, so I'm handing this over to you now. Is that okay?

Freja: Ooh, yes, please. Does this mean it's my turn to ask you the scary questions now?

Me: Bring it on.

Commentary:
There's a moment in every good candidate conversation where the guard drops and the real chat kicks in. Banter's allowed, honesty's welcome, and nobody's pretending to be more polished than they are. That's where we're at now. No treading on eggshells, just a grown-up chat with a dash of sarcasm and a decent Wi-Fi signal.

Freja: Cool. Well, I'm going to start with the salary. According to the details you sent, it's up to £65,000. How will they feel about me already being on £70k? And, realistically, Pureline might try offering me another £5k to keep me. That's a lot of money to walk away from. Do you think I'm too overpriced for them?

Commentary:
Salary's the bit everyone dances around, usually while silently panicking. If she's bringing this up now, it means we've hit a good level of trust. My job? To stop her spiralling and give her the facts, without

sounding like I'm rolling them in glitter.

Me: I get why you're asking. There's always that little voice that says, am I pushing my luck here? But no, I don't think you're overpriced. I know there's flexibility on this. Let me explain. Nordalyn was initially advertising this at £45k. They had no real sense of what the market looked like. After becoming involved, I visited them, conducted some research, and demonstrated that the industry average was actually closer to £65k. They had to go back to finance and the head office, but when they saw what it was costing them not to have someone in place, they adjusted it. There's room to go above that for the right person, if we can justify the value. Which we can in spades.

Freja: That puts my mind at rest, thank you. What about a bonus or commission? Is that paid annually?

Me: Nope. Quarterly, uncapped, and entirely based on what you deliver. They're estimating you could pull in another £7.5k per quarter with an on-target performance. However, as the sales cycles are quite lengthy, it might take six months before that filters through to you.

Freja: That's understandable, and also very generous. Are people already earning that kind of money?

Me: Yes, though not in your sector. The sales team is split across divisions, and the food sector is relatively new. But the exciting bit: the same product launched in Germany and the US, and they are crushing it over there. Their teams are six months in and absolutely flying. As part of the interview process, you'll have the opportunity to speak with them off the record. Ask them anything you want about targets, earnings, and what life on the road's like. No filters.

Freja: Seriously? That's pretty rare. But yes, I'd love that. It would help me understand how realistic it all is. Do you know how much travel I'd be doing? Like, how often would I be staying away from home?

Me: I know the patch is UK-wide, but I'll be honest, they don't know the exact number of overnight stays. What I do know is that the first six months are going to be... lively.

Freja: Why's that?

Me: Because they're sitting on around £800,000 worth of warm leads generated through marketing in Denmark, but they don't have anyone with food sector knowledge in the UK to close them. It's just sitting there, gathering dust.

Freja: You mean all that business is just going untouched? That actually makes me feel a bit sick.

Commentary:
This is where you sit back and let the candidate sell themselves on the job. I didn't need to pitch a thing; her reaction did all the heavy lifting. A well-timed pause can be more powerful than any sales pitch.

Me: Yeah, me too. Darren and a couple of others have been trying to cover it, but they're winging it, completely outside their comfort zone. They don't speak food. So yes, it'll likely involve overnight stays at first. How would that sit with your home setup?

Freja: It sounds like what I'm doing now anyway. I cover Ireland, so I'm away a couple of nights a month already. We have a solid system at home; his family helps, and my husband's great with our daughter. I'd need to chat with him in more detail, but... honestly? It sounds like something I could get my teeth into. I can't believe they're leaving that money on the table. I'm guessing I'd be working for Darren. What's he like?

Me: Yes, you'd report to Darren. He's a bit of a reluctant hero, if I'm honest.

Freja: Reluctant. How?

Commentary:
Clients like Darren are everywhere: loyal, overloaded, and quietly

desperate for someone to step in and fix the mess. The trick is to find candidates who see that as a challenge, not a red flag. Freja didn't flinch.

Me: He's stepped up because no one else would. Been with the company for over 12 years, but always in other divisions. He's sharp, loyal, and knows the business, but food isn't his thing, and he knows it. This role gives him a bit of a headache. If you asked him off the record, I reckon he'd love someone to take it off his hands completely.

Freja: Now you're talking. That's exactly what I want, that level of ownership. And to be fair, he sounds a lot like my current boss.

Me: Oh, right? How do you feel about that?

Freja: I'm used to it. Most senior managers in engineering or manufacturing come from the same mould. My clients are the same. I know how to manage it. What's the interview process like?

Me: The first step is a video call with Darren; he's flexible on the timing. Then, you'll have the opportunity to have an informal chat with someone from the German or US team. Totally optional. No feedback from them to Darren. It's just for you. If everything looks good, the next step would be a face-to-face interview in Derby. That's likely to include a presentation and one of the Directors sitting in. How do you usually feel about interviews?

Freja: Nervous. I'm out of practice. I know I can do the job; I just hope I can convey that effectively.

Commentary:
This is where most recruiters will go, "You'll be great! You've got this!" But what she needed was realism; just hearing "I get it" is the most reassuring thing you can say.

Me: That makes total sense. And funnily enough, you're not the only one feeling that way. When I spoke to Darren about the interview process, he mentioned that he dislikes interviews as well. He told me they make him feel awkward and overly formal. So,

I offered to draft a few questions in advance, just to help him keep it natural and get what he needs from the conversation. I could do the same for you. Would that make things feel a bit easier for you?

Commentary:
I offered the same thing to Darren so that he could humanise it. Everyone's better when they're not in panic mode. Interviews are weird enough without turning them into a performance.

Freja: Yes, that sounds like a plan. Thank you.

Me: I'll make sure you are supported and well-informed throughout the process. Imagine, for a second, that all this goes to plan; you've had the interviews. You've got the offer. You're in. What would need to be happening six months into the role for you to look back and say, "Yes, I absolutely made the right move"?

Freja: Six months in? I'd want the lead pipeline cleared, nothing sitting around gathering dust. Everything would be either closed, progressed, or parked with purpose. I'd have brought in at least two major projects and be well on my way to taking ownership of the division, not just managing accounts, but shaping where it's heading. That's the role I've been visualising. That's where I want to be.

Commentary:
That's when you know: she's not visualising the interview anymore, she's imagining the impact.

Me: That's crystal clear, and honestly, Freja, I can see you there already. It's not just what you've said, it's how you've said it. This isn't a whim for you. It's measured. How would you like to move forward with this?

Freja: I'd like you to speak to Darren and let him know I'm keen to take the next step.

Me: I know this isn't a light decision. Leaving somewhere after seven years never is. But I can hear the excitement in your voice. You've weighed it up, and that says a lot about your courage. It feels like the right opportunity, at the right time, for the right reasons.

Freja: Yes, I have a great feeling about this.

Next Steps

Me: That's great. So, here's what happens next: First, I'll put together a profile for you, something that captures your value and the difference you could make at Nordalyn. I'll send you a copy first so feel free to tweak. I'll then speak to Darren. Depending on how that goes, I might also loop in Amber, the HR Manager. She'll know more about the policy around overnight travel, That might just fast-track this a little. Once Darren has your profile, I'll initiate the first stage. Does that sound okay to you?

Freja: Sounds perfect. Thank you.

Final Commentary:
And there it is. She didn't need any persuasion; she needed the room to picture herself on the inside. Once she made the decision, it came from her, not me. That's the sweet spot, when a candidate asks you to move things forward because it feels like their idea, their timing, their choice. My job now is simple: capture her story cleanly, take it to Darren, and make sure nothing gets lost in translation.

Let's see how this pans out in Part Three.

The Candidate Rap-Up

In the Flow

Yo, she came in cool, with her cards held tight,
Talkin' numbers and nerves, kept questions light.
But beneath that calm, there was fire and fight,
A woman on the edge of takin' flight.

She crushed the doubts, didn't dance or sway,
Said, "If I go in, I'm leadin' the way."
No sugar-coatin', no need to perform,
She's built for the storm, not just to conform.

She spotted the gaps, saw the cash on the floor,
Didn't flinch at the travel or the targets in store.
And when I said, "You in?", she didn't delay,
Just nodded and said, "Let's do it, today."

Peace out... **The Clean Soul way**

Part Two Summary:

Closing Reflections

And that's the loop closed on Part Two. Our qualifying calls have all been done. We've walked with the client, dug beneath the job description, and sat in the fire with the candidate. None of it was quick or tidy, but that's the job. Recruitment done properly is never neat. What matters is that each stage was approached with curiosity, patience, and the belief that people deserve more than a pitch-slap. Heavy-handed persuasion or manipulation no longer cuts through. Our market is far too savvy for that.

For most recruiters, speed is the name of the game. We submit a CV, arrange an interview, and hope something sticks.

What you've just seen in Part Two isn't luck or chance. It's the Triple E Journey in action. Each stage keeps us anchored, each one building on the last.

Exploration showed us where things stand today and what's missing. It opened up loyalty, frustration, ambition, and the gap between them.

Evaluation held up a mirror to the realities of the obstacles they could face, the weight of real life: family pressures, loyalty ties, unspoken fears of change.

Expectations finally shifted the lens forward. We tested what success might look like, not in theory, but in six-month visions, in pay conversations, in the rhythms of daily life.

Together, those three steps kept the conversation from drifting into small talk or collapsing into a pitch. They gave the client, the job, and the candidate equal footing. Value uncovered, resistance explored, and expectations aligned. Each dynamic was tested on its own terms, using the three core principles throughout.

Now we're ready for Part Three. This is where the lines cross. Client, job, and candidate information are no longer kept in separate conversations. They collide, overlap, and test each other. The art is not just about handling each piece, but about managing the relationship between them.

That's the journey ahead: weaving three separate strands into one process, one story, one outcome.

If you've ever worked a desk, you'll know why the Triple E matters, because spray and pray isn't a strategy, hope is not a process, and crossing your fingers has never once counted as stakeholder engagement.

PART THREE

BOARDING PASS

FLIGHT NUMBER
RWACS303

PASSENGER(S)
CLIENT CANDIDATE JOB

DESTINATION
OFFERLAND

STATUS
CLEARED FOR TAKE-OFF

Boarding Call

Clean Soul Flight 303 Now Departing

Ladies and gentlemen, welcome aboard Clean Soul Airlines. This is your captain speaking. Fasten your seatbelts, because from this point on, we're flying three-relational.

Clients, jobs, and candidates are no longer on separate flights; they're squeezed into the same cabin, knees knocking, tray tables down, trying to get to the same destination without a mid-air scrap.

Our first leg takes us to Candidate Presentation, where the carefully built story is delivered to the client, baggage checked, value declared, nothing lost in transit.

Next stop: Interview Preparation, where the conversations take off, the nerves hit turbulence, and a calm recruiter keeps the drinks trolley upright.

Debriefs, where things get a little steamy!

Final approach: Offerland, where every decision made along the way comes into land. The runway is short, the crosswinds are strong, but if we've done our job right, we'll touch down smoothly.

Please ensure all outdated playbooks are powered down, emotional baggage is stowed safely in the overhead locker, and the three dynamics are strapped in side by side.

This is recruitment done relationally, not transactionally, and it's about to get lively.

Cabin crew, lock the doors. Flight 303 is ready for take-off.

Chapter 11

Candidate Presentation

CV Attached

Well, we've been on a journey, haven't we? We've tackled winning over a prospect, taking on a job, and qualifying a candidate.

This whole journey started because I had sent a "How are things going?" message to a candidate I once had in a recruitment process some years back. Tony, now working as Operations Director for Nordalyn, suggested that I speak with Amber, the HR Manager, as she was having trouble finding candidates.

Moral: Keep your clients close and your network closer.

All three elements of the recruitment dynamic centred on those initial qualifying calls. I focused on this stage because it's where we tend to make the most mistakes. It's where data gets burned, where frustration brews, where people ghost us, lie to us, or vanish into the recruitment abyss.

Now, you might be sitting there thinking: "*Yeah, right. These scripts are way too polished. It never goes this smoothly.*" It's a fair point.

However, every one of these examples has been rooted in real-life situations. The names have changed, and a few red flags have been sprinkled in. But the bones? The bones are true. I've kept the same scenario consistent throughout so we can properly follow the journey. And yes, I made it look like a seamless dream because I wanted you to see what's possible.

I wanted to show you:

- How the mindset I was operating from makes a difference.
- How relationships were built, not thinly disguised rapport.
- How the right questions got people thinking about their internal world.
- How I never had to persuade, manipulate, boast, or claim I was the best.

When you operate from trust, depth, and integrity, you increase productivity without burning through data. This is how you elevate our reputation and your brand.

We've done the hard part: the initial calls, which took a bit of unpicking, but recruitment doesn't stop there. We're here to make money too, and the journey continues.

I'm not going to promise a fairy tale ending, but we will follow through on every key touchpoint between now and the outcome. And yes, our colourful cast of characters, plus a few new ones, will be making a return.

Update From My Last Call with Freja

We have not long finished our chat. To refresh your memory, we had a phone call to gauge her interest in the role and then met on video to discuss the value she could bring and whether the job would be a good fit for her. We are now on Day Two since our initial call.

I have put together a profile for her that she has approved, and now it's time to present her to the company.

That means my job shifts again. I'm no longer just discovering value or unpicking blind spots. I'm now threading the story together: Freja's achievements, Darren's demands, Amber's influence, and Nordalyn's ambitions. If any part is left dangling, the whole thing risks stalling before it leaves the ground.

Which is why I didn't march straight to Darren. His fuse is short, his pride runs deep, and nothing kills momentum faster than a poorly timed "no." The first stop is Amber, my inside track.

Me: Amber, have I caught you at a bad time for an off-the-record chat about a candidate for the TSE role?

Amber: Off the record? I'm intrigued. Go on.

Me: Thanks. She's a technical sales pro with a food sector background, selling capital kits, engineering qualifications, and having built her patch from scratch. She ticks all Darren's boxes, but I wanted to flag some things before presenting her to him.

Amber: You had me at "she." That in itself is a rarity. Send me her CV?

Me: Are you by your laptop? I'll ping it now. Please take a look while I waffle about the weather.

[Pause]

Amber: Oh my god! She's Danish.

Me: Yep. Moved here in 2018 and married a Brit. She knows Nordalyn and has heard some good things about the PMH system. How do you think Darren would feel about her Danish roots?

Amber: Head Office will love it. I might be wrong, but Darren may feel threatened by it.

Me: Really? I thought he'd be glad to hand some pressure back.

Amber: He is, but she's the complete package. They might prefer her in charge, which could ruffle him. Plus, her salary is over budget.

Me: That's precisely why I came to you first. She earns £70k basic plus a £10k bonus. If she resigns, they'll probably offer another £5k to keep her.

Amber: Yes, she has "counteroffer" written all over her. Do you think she would use us as leverage?

Commentary:
This is where I usually get twitchy. But I've learned that calling the red flags early makes tackling them easier. I'd rather plant the seed now than let Darren trip over it later.

Me: Counteroffers are always a risk with people like her. From the conversations I've had with her, she seemed pretty genuine. However, she was head-hunted last year by a direct competitor, and Pureline didn't want to lose her. What drove that at the time was the fact that they were not innovating their products, whereas the competition was. They made some promises at the time to address the issue, but no action has been taken so far.

Amber: Why is she looking for a new role?

Me: She's not actively looking, but I reached out to her. Although she receives numerous recruiter reach-outs, she was very taken with the Nordalyn products. How do you think we should position her to Darren to justify a higher budget?

Amber: Considering her accomplishments, current role, and experience starting from scratch, I think Darren will see that straight away.

Me: That's good to know. Apart from her ability to generate new business, it's also worth noting that she handles tenders, bids, audits, and project management of installations, so she has the potential to save on another headcount.

Amber: Wow, how does she fit it all in? Typically, we would contract the PM stuff, so that's worth knowing. So far, she's looking a bit too good to be true. How does she come across?

Me: I'm not being biased here, but her communication skills are top-notch. She's very engaging. I can see why she has done so well. However, there is one thing that may be a problem.

Amber: Oh dear, go on.

Me: She has a 3-year-old daughter and currently covers the UK and Ireland. She usually stays away from home several times a month, but if it is any more than that, she would need plenty of notice to arrange childcare. She just likes to put her to bed at night.

Amber: That's understandable, and Head Office is very pro-family. She is also responsible for her own diary, so I can't see that as a deal-breaker. I'm due to have a meeting with Darren this afternoon. Would you like me to run things past him to gauge his reaction? We should strike while the iron's hot.

Me: That will be great. Could you please let me know what he says?

Commentary:
Amber didn't just get it; she was already lining up the argument I needed Darren to hear. Mission accomplished. Now it was time to let things percolate.

Don't mind me… I'm just updating the CRM… Ooh, hello, Darren's calling me. Two hours, that's all it took.

Either Amber gave him the hard sell, or the phrase "Danish engineer with chilled food experience" triggered a primal response.

Let's find out which.

Darren: Right, I've had a chat with Amber, and I've just seen Freja's CV. Very interesting profile. How soon can we see her?

Me: That's encouraging. What was it you found interesting?

Darren: Well, she's Danish, loads of sales experience in the food sector, capital equipment background… It's as if she were created in a lab just for us. But that salary, she's on seventy grand? Plus a bonus? That's a bit spicy.

Me: I figured that might raise an eyebrow. They'll likely offer her another five grand to stay if she resigns. How would you present her to the powers that be, so that the value she can bring outweighs the uplift in budget?

Darren: Depending on how she performs at the interview, I'd take it straight to Head Office. It helps that she's Danish and can demonstrate her ability to overachieve. But come on, what's to stop her from rinsing us for an offer and using it to squeeze more from her lot?

Commentary:
Ah, yes, the recruiter's rite of passage. The "she's just using us for leverage" speech. If I had a tenner for every time I've heard it, I could afford to uplift the counteroffer myself.

Me: Fair question. I've had two long conversations with her. She's not shopping around, and she wasn't even looking. It was the PMH she seemed to buy into. She's intrigued, not desperate. There's a difference.

Darren: But how do we keep her intrigued? How do we make sure she stays in the boat?

Me: Paint her a vision of the future, one with challenge and growth. She wants something new to believe in. She also feels a genuine debt of gratitude towards Pureline; they took a gamble on her, and she doesn't forget that.

Darren: Yes, Amber told me about that. Fair play to how she went about it; she's got something about her. What would you say her knowledge of maintenance systems is like?

Me: She's not had direct experience with them, no. However, she has spent the last seven years on the shop floor, so she's well aware of the impact of downtime in food operations. Given her background with high-spec kit, how long do you think she'd need to get up to speed?

Darren: Honestly? I think she'd pick it up quickly. She'll have to go to Denmark anyway for two weeks, but I reckon she could be up to speed sooner than that. I understand she's got a little girl. How would she manage time away, or would we need to bring the training here?

Commentary:
Notice that? He is already trying to make things easier for her.

Me: Yes, she's aware of the training and open to it. I reckon she'd jump at the chance to return to Denmark, but she'll need to work through the logistics. I only finished speaking to her this morning, so she's still processing quite a bit.

Darren: Fair enough. We'll cross that bridge if and when we come to it. So, when do you think she'll be up for a Teams interview?

Me: Leaving Pureline is a big decision, and she'll want to chat with her husband first. Would you be free to meet her on Friday, the day after tomorrow?

Darren: Yeah, that's fine. Best not to railroad her too quickly. See if 11 o'clock would be doable; if not, I'll work around her.

Me: Perfect. And what are you hoping to cover in the interview?

Darren: I'll explain what we're trying to achieve and give her more information about the product line. I can see her figures on the CV, but I'll want to dig into those. Don't worry, I'm not going to scare her off. I thought those questions you sent through were good, and I've learned my lesson.

Me: That's good to hear. I'll message her to say you'd like to set this up, and we'll have a catch-up tomorrow. Thanks, Darren.

Darren: You've done well with this one. If you get any more CVs like hers, just call me.

Commentary:
Darren was sold. He was already picturing her in the role, which meant one thing: it was time to introduce Freja into the loop.

Pre-Message Commentary

Things are moving fast. Too fast. Maybe Freja's going to feel overwhelmed?

We'd only spoken for the first time yesterday. She'd barely had time to sleep on it, let alone fully picture the change. I don't want to push, not now. But with Darren already rearranging his diary, I needed to test the water.

WhatsApp Messages

Me – Freja:
Hi, Nordalyn loved your profile. I know it's short notice, but they would like to do a Teams interview with you this Friday at 11.00 am. Would that work for you?

Freja – Me:
Wow. Speedy work. Yes, timings all good.

Me – Freja:
Cool. Would love to do a prep call tomorrow. Could you fit that in?

Freja – Me:
9.30 after the nursery run would be great. THKS

Before I move on, I dropped Amber a quick email, thanking her for softening up the boss. Interview confirmations were sent to both Darren and Freja.

Closing Summary

Ladies and gentlemen, Freja has now boarded. Seatbelt fastened, tray table stowed, but we're still on the tarmac. The next leg involves interviews, including preparation, briefs, and debriefs, along with the occasional bit of turbulence.

Cabin crew, secure the passengers. We're cleared for Chapter 12.

Candidate Presentation Rap-up

The Runway

Yo, I dropped her profile, neat and tight
Amber gave the nod, said, "Yeah, that's right."
Darren took a peek, tried to play it cool,
But two hours later, he was breaking the rule.

He's sold on the numbers, the Danish name,
Spicy salary talk, same old game.
But behind the doubts, the penny dropped:
This ain't a maybe, it's a hire that popped.

Freja's on board, the diary's set,
Teams call Friday, best one yet.
From whisper to pitch in a day or two,
That's how we roll with the **Clean Soul Crew.**

Chapter 12

The Interview Brief

Prep, Panic, and the Myth of Candidate Readiness

We like to think it's a quick ten-minute job, a checklist. "Have you looked at their website?" "Do you know who's interviewing you?" "Got your suit ready?" Tick, tick, tick, and off you pop.

But here's what I've learned after 25 years of watching what happens between "yes" and "interview confirmed": this is where the wobbles hit. This is the moment they sit on the sofa, take a breath, and say out loud: "What the hell am I doing?" It's where the panic kicks in. The "what ifs." The "am I good enough." The "can I leave my job, my team, my safety net?"

And yet, we treat it like admin; a quick call, a few instructions, and a few bullet points.

This part of the process is critical. Everything, for the candidate, the client, and you, is an unknown quantity at this stage. You don't know how the conversation will unfold. They don't know how they'll be received, and the client doesn't know what's walking through their (virtual) door.

Conducted carelessly, interview preparation can lead to failure or, worse, complete disengagement. But done with care, concern, and integrity? It becomes a lifeline, a chance to steady the nerves, re-centre the motivation, and build just enough confidence to be themselves. The person in control of this process isn't us, it's them, and if they don't feel ready, emotionally, practically, or mentally, the interview either won't happen or will go tits-up.

So, no predictions here, no assumptions. Just a conversation. One human to another. That's what this part of the process is really for, and that's what we're about to do.

Questions to Avoid

The interview briefing should be one of the most valuable conversations we have with candidates. Yet too often, it slips into a string of reminders that could just as easily be sent by email: "Have you researched the company?" "Do you know where you're going?" "Don't forget to discuss your accomplishments." It's well-meaning, but it reduces the briefing to logistics instead of building confidence.

What candidates really need is the chance to think through how they'll handle the conversation and what would help them feel ready. That means moving away from routine reminders and asking questions that prompt them to reflect for themselves. Here are a few examples.

AVOID: Have you researched the company?
REPLACE: What have you noticed about this company that feels relevant to you?

AVOID: What questions will you ask them?
REPLACE: What would you want to learn in the interview, so you can get a feel for whether the role is right for you?

AVOID: Don't forget to tell them about your achievements?
REPLACE: How do you plan to highlight the areas where you can add value?

With those reframes in place, the interview briefing stops being a set of reminders and becomes a chance for the candidate to step into the room prepared, confident, and in control. The calls that follow illustrate how that difference is reflected in honest conversations.

Interview Prep

Me: Hi, Freja, thank you for taking the time to chat today. I know it's been a bit high-octane the last couple of days, so I just wanted to check in before we go any further... Has anything shifted since we last spoke?

Freja: (slightly hesitant) Umm... not shifted, exactly. I'm still interested and want to proceed. It's just... well, I had a proper chat with my husband last night. He asked a few questions about making this sort of change, when everything is going smoothly where I am.

Me: Ah, okay. That's fair. What sort of things came up?

Freja: Just the practical side. He asked if it would be more than what I'm doing now, and I didn't have an answer. I mean, I stay away maybe two or three nights a month at the moment, and that works, but if it was going to be more... I don't know. It caught me off guard a bit.

Me: That makes a lot of sense, and it's an entirely valid concern, especially with a little one at home. Changing jobs after seven years is likely to cause some disruption to your family life. What do you think you would need to get out of the interview tomorrow to feel more assured that the risks of going ahead could be minimised?

Commentary:
And there it is: the wobble. Stakeholders, partners, or loved ones who are not aligned or on board with this major decision can derail everything. It's surfaced early, and whilst there is nothing I can do about it, persuasion won't work, all I can be is supportive. At least she can now start factoring this into her decision-making process. If it does derail, then at least I'm aware that it could happen.

Freja: I would like to know what my day-to-day responsibilities will involve, and for them to recognise that I am a mother too.

Me: Of course, that's a great start. I spoke to Amber, the HR Manager, yesterday. She confirmed the role is very much self-managed.

No one's expecting you to live out of a suitcase. She also mentioned that Nordalyn, being Danish, has a very pro-family identity. It's similar to how you work now; you'd be in control of your diary.

Commentary:
I could've just said "it's fine, don't worry", but that wouldn't cut it. Reassurance without evidence is just noise. She needed details. Permission. Context. Otherwise, the doubt lingers.

Freja: (relieved) Oh, okay. That helps. I think I just panicked a bit when he asked. Like I suddenly realised I was excited... but hadn't stopped to process any of it.

Me: You've had a lot come at you in a short space of time. You didn't go looking for this; it came to you. So it's okay to feel a bit unsettled. How are you feeling about the interview tomorrow?

Freja: Yeah. I still really like the sound of the company, the product, and everything. I just feel... I don't know... a bit nervous now.

Me: Again, that's very normal. Darren will be nervous too. The primary purpose of this is to explore whether it might be a good fit for both of you. Have you given any thought to the type of questions you would like to ask him?

Freja: Yes, I had a read of the questions you sent over. They were excellent. I want to ask him about a million things. I am primarily interested in learning more about the products, the types of customers they target, and their current approach to managing incoming leads. I particularly like the one about how they plan on measuring my success in the role. What did they like about my CV?

Me: They thought your skillset and experience seemed perfect for them. What stood out, though, was your Danish roots. They believe this will be a massive help to them in terms of communication and will alleviate some of the pressure on Darren.

Freja: Oh, that is interesting. I suppose understanding the Danes' operations and culture would make the role easier. What did they make of my salary expectations? Is this likely to be an issue for them?

Me: I had a very frank conversation with both Darren and Amber about this and why it is higher than average. Darren thought it was a bit spicy but felt his best course of action would be obtaining sign-off directly from Head Office by justifying that the value you bring would outweigh what the initial costs would be.

Commentary:
Talking about money is always the tension point. If you shy away from it, so will they. If you rush it, they'll retreat. This was the moment to reinforce her worth, not negotiate on her behalf.

Freja: That's a relief. I'm just not sure how to convey it, so I don't sound too expensive to them if they bring up my salary expectations.

Me: If salary comes up, just ground it in results, not in need. You're not asking for a handout. You're offering a track record. What would you want him to know about your successes?

Freja: The wins I've had in the chilled food sector and the tender conversions.

Me: Agreed. Those aren't just numbers; they speak about your work ethic. You've consistently exceeded target, managed end-to-end project delivery, and built a client base from scratch. How comfortable will you be if he asks you about your client base and who the people are, given that this happened in another interview you had?

Freja: To be fair, I'm a bit sceptical, but since they're not our competitors, even if they went after them, it wouldn't hurt me.

Me: Good, and remember, you're interviewing them just as much as they're interviewing you.

Commentary:
I could feel her relaxing now. The energy was different, slower, steadier. We weren't just prepping for an interview. We were un-

tangling the emotion underneath it. This was about helping her find her own confidence.

Me: What else do you think you need support with for tomorrow?

Freja: I think I feel okay now; you've put my mind at rest.

Me: That's good to know. Darren will be the one working overtime to impress you tomorrow. I think you just have to be you. What outcome are you hoping for at the end of the interview?

Freja: I want him to explore the possibility of moving to the next stage, hopefully face-to-face, and I believe this would be a good opportunity for me.

Me: Brilliant. And if you feel it is right for you, have you planned how you will likely approach this with Pureline, should they make an offer?

Freja: I've been thinking about it a lot. I'm very nervous about it because my boss there is also a friend, so it would need careful handling.

Me: Let's see what tomorrow holds for you and check again once I have your feedback. We can then work out the best approach together. Just remember, this has to be right for you and your family. If anything shifts before tomorrow, or you feel differently when you wake up, that's okay. Just let me know. No pressure, only what feels right.

Freja: Thank you. You have been really helpful. I will give you a call straight after to let you know how it goes.

Final Commentary:

She's ready, but not because I fired off ten tips and a LinkedIn stalk list. She's ready because we aired the doubts, checked what mattered, and slowed it down enough for her to feel like she was still in control.

Interview Prep Rap-Up

Prepping the Pitch

Yo, Freja had the jitters, the late-night chat,
Husband playing devil's advocate, fancy that.
Not a pep talk, prep, or a PowerPoint plan,
Just me with my notes and a Clean Soul scan.

Questions packed tighter than a Ryanair seat,
Ready for Darren when the Teams link beeped.
We saw off the doubts, kept panic at bay,
Turned nerves to ammo in a recruiter's way.

It's not about polish or LinkedIn spam,
It's prepping with people, that's the **Clean Soul jam.**

Chapter 13

Interview Feedback

From Buzz to Balance: The Debrief that Matters

What's your opening gambit when you speak to a candidate after their interview?

Is it "How did it go?"

It's a natural question, a curious one. You're trying to get a read on how they feel. The problem is: it rarely opens the right door.

Most of the time, the response will be something like:

I think it went okay.
"The hiring manager was a bit hard to read."
"Not sure, they didn't give much away."
"I don't think I nailed it."
"It was the best interview I've ever had!" (This is the scenario we will be dealing with in the feedback call, and it's not all roses and rainbows.)

There is nothing wrong with these responses; it's just that after an interview, candidates find it difficult to articulate how the interview went, and there's a reason for this...

A first interview is a lot like a blind date. You're meeting someone for the first time. You've Googled them, you've picked your outfit carefully, and you're trying to strike that impossible balance between confident, humble, clever, relatable, credible, and hireable.

It's not just tiring; it's exhausting. You walk out of that meeting a hot-wired blob of adrenaline and static, trying to remember if you smiled too much, talked too fast, or missed the moment to say the one thing that matters.

And now here we are, asking them to summarise it all in a three-second soundbite.

So yes, "*How did it go?*" is a fair question, but it's not a helpful one.

Not if we're trying to move the process forward or get to the very heart of it.

What they need from us in that moment isn't another bog-standard, vanilla question. They need questions that will help them make sense of what they have just been through, away from being judged or scrutinised on their performance.

It's about whether the role fits who they are and what they need.

That's why the usual debrief questions miss the mark. Instead of a quick headline answer, we need questions that help them unpack the experience and weigh up what it means for them. Here are some examples.

Questions to Avoid

AVOID: How did it go?
REPLACE: How did the role match up to what you expected?

AVOID: What questions did they ask you?
REPLACE: What questions would you answer differently, if you had another chance?

AVOID: Would you accept the job if offered?
REPLACE: What would you need more clarity on to consider the role a viable option?

AVOID: Where else are you interviewing at the moment?
REPLACE: How will you decide which would be the best opportunity for you?

AVOID: Any concerns?
REPLACE: What areas of the role would you need more understanding on?

These questions take them out of performance mode and into reflection mode. It brings the focus back to alignment, not approval.

Our job is to interpret. If they feel unsure, let them express it; if something feels off, help them explore the issue; if they're swept up in excitement, check what's driving it.

This is the point where emotions intersect with decision-making, and if we don't slow things down here, we risk steering people down the wrong path.

Freja Debrief call

Commentary:
Her interview was booked for 11:00. It's now 12:53. By recruiter maths, that's 38 minutes past the "She's either ghosted or being offered champagne" mark.

Do I call? Tempting, but no. Always best to let them call first, unless you enjoy sounding like a clingy date.

Still... she said it was scheduled for an hour, and now it's creeping towards one. Either the whole thing went off track, or something went very, very right.

1:05 pm. Phone rings. Freja.

She's breathless, euphoric, and almost apologetic, in a sorry, not sorry sort of way.

Freja: Oh my god, sorry, sorry, sorry. The interview has only just finished. It ran way over. I didn't want it to end. I've got so much to tell you. I bet you thought I was ghosting you.

Me: Hi, Freja. I wasn't panicking. (I so was.) I think you need to take a breath, though. It sounds like it went well. How did the job line up to what you were expecting it to be?

Freja: It beat all the expectations I had of it. We talked about everything, literally everything. He even took me through their plans for Trenatek. I didn't expect that at all.

Me: Trenatek? Is that a new product?

Freja: Oh no, I was wondering why you hadn't mentioned it. Nordalyn is setting up the PMH product as a separate company, still under their umbrella. There will be numerous growth opportunities there. It's probably all hush-hush, but they are in the throes of putting it in place in the UK now. I can't tell you how excited I am.

Commentary:
You might have thought Darren would have mentioned a tiny little detail like this humongous selling point. Entirely my bad for not finding this out earlier.

[Phone buzzes in my hand. Missed call from Darren.]

Me: Hang on, speak of the devil. Darren's just tried to call me.

Freja: (laughs) Call him back. I'm desperate for a wee, a cuppa, and food.

Me: Yes, it sounds like you need to sort that out. I will find out what he has to say and give you an hour to grab a bite and catch your breath.

Freja: Thank you, an hour will be good. I want to know everything he says.

Commentary:
Never ask anyone questions when they need to use the loo, need a drink, or are hungry. Listening to how excited she was and the way she was talking, it would be best for her to catch hold of her thoughts.

I barely had time to boil the kettle before Darren was back on the line. Which, in Darren's language, means something big just clicked.

Darren's Feedback

Me: Sorry, Darren, I was speaking to Freja. She knew you were trying to call me, so we've agreed to talk in a short while.

Darren: What did she have to say?

Me: We didn't have much time, but she seemed super excited, though, and was speaking ten to the dozen.

Darren: Yes, she can talk, can't she?

Me: She reminds me of you a bit. Were the questions I suggested you ask her any good?

Darren: I don't know, I didn't have to use them. It was all very natural. I got on with her like a house on fire. She's perfect, the full package. I think we should move forward with this and submit an offer to her before someone else does.

Commentary:
Did Darren just mention the O word? No back and forth, no negotiations, no messing around. Just a bloody offer. Off one virtual interview. The gods of recruitment are shining down on me today. Whoop-de-do.

Take a breath, Zandy!

It's hard not to get excited, isn't it? What we are witnessing is interview infatuation. Two people instantly hit it off, like they had known each other for years. They both feel it's "right" and, on occasion, it is. But when the offer goggles come off, when they stop and think, "ooh, I didn't know I'd be travelling that much," or that endearing, engaging personality is masking a high-maintenance control freak, then things can turn sour pretty quickly.

Now we all know a little about Freja. She is more than likely talking to her husband right now. She is super animated and highly excitable as she tells him how fantastic the interview went. Now, he could be the most supportive partner in the world, but he is going to be thinking, "*Who's this geezer, lighting up my missus this way?*" If this is rushed through, then he will do everything in his power to stop it from happening. We need to breathe. We need to assess the impacts and start managing expectations.

Me: Oh wow, that sounds like it went really well, and making an offer off the back of one interview is brilliant, but how would you plan to factor in any last-minute wobbles?

Darren: But she loved it. She said she was excited. We should strike while the iron's hot, keep the momentum going.

Me: Exactly, she's excited, but it's still raw. She needs time to process, to talk to her husband, and figure out what this means for her family. If you throw an offer at her now, it'll feel like pressure, not opportunity.

Darren: Hmmm. I suppose.

Me: You would be asking her to make a massive, life-changing decision on the spot. Out of interest, what sort of offer would you be making to her to ensure that Pureline won't be able to counter?

Darren: She was asking for £75,000. Do you think they would still counter on that?

Me: Without a doubt. Who have you spoken to so far about getting sign-off on something that's already ten K over budget?

Darren: No one yet, I haven't had the chance, but there won't be a problem with that. How much more do you think Pureline would offer?

Me: I don't know, but I do know that she is more motivated by the products, the opportunity, and being at the start of this journey. Now she mentioned Trenatek to me. I've only just heard of it, so I'm wondering if she could be more instrumental in managing the company, perhaps in a more senior position than she's currently in? Something Pureline could not compete with?

Darren: (Silence) Erm. That's something to think about.

Me: Could you see her being able to do something more senior?

Darren: Hands down, she could do it, but it's not the role we are recruiting for. I'm not sure if Head Office would consider it.

Me: I know, it's a long shot. What would be the situation if you were to deliver an offer right now, and then there was back and forth with a counteroffer, and she ultimately pulled out?

Darren: Back to square one, I guess, but there is no way I want to lose her. You've set the bar very high with her, and no one is going to come up to scratch in comparison. So, I'm ready to pull out the big guns. What would you suggest?

Me: Very wise, and you're right; I haven't come across anyone near her standards so far, so I think it would be a good move to fight for her. My advice would be to set up another stage, with Head Office. Either get them over here or pay for her to go there. Let them see first-hand what a diamond she is and how she can demonstrate her value in person.

Darren: Yes, that's good. Perhaps we could cover the costs for her and her family to attend. Her parents live quite near Nordalyn's, so we could make it a family trip. Look, I'll get on the phone with them straight after this. Call Freja back and sound her out for a potential offer, see if she's really on board, and then we'll talk later to see where we go from here.

Final Commentary:
This is where the job of a recruiter pivots from messenger to mediator. Darren's head was already halfway to the finish line, pen poised over a contract. But recruitment isn't a sprint, it's a relay. If I let him dash now, he'd trip over the baton of a counteroffer, or worse, a husband's quiet veto.

Slowing him down gave him room to think, and look what happened. His mind jumped from "*let's lock her in*" to "*How do we elevate this into something Pureline could never match?*"

Freja Follow-Up Call:

Post-Interview Debrief & Expectation Setting

It's been an hour since Freja's euphoric download. She's had time to eat, breathe, and, most importantly, talk to her husband. The adrenaline would have faded by now. This next call wasn't just about feedback. It was about checking what had surfaced once the buzz wore off.

Me: Hi, Freja, how are you feeling now you've had a bit of time to decompress?

Freja: Yes, I'm a bit more grounded now, so we can have a proper conversation instead of me sounding like I'd just won the lottery. Tell me what Darren said.

Me: Well, he was as excited about it as you were. Said you were the complete package. He was impressed and is keen to take things forward, based on how you feel about it. How did your husband react to your excitement?

Freja: What! How did you know I spoke to him?

Me: Because whenever anyone has a good interview, they cannot wait to tell their loved ones. It's a natural reaction. How was he?

Commentary:
It's never just the candidate you're recruiting. There's a board of unseen stakeholders in the background, partners, parents, and even the family dog. This is where the offer goggles start to fog up.

Freja: It was a bit weird. He is usually very supportive and makes the right noises, but he seems nervous about me leaving my job for something else.

Me: That's very understandable; it's a lot to get your head around. He wasn't in the interview and probably doesn't understand all the implications just yet. What do you think would put his mind at ease?

Freja: I think I just need to convince him that I would still have the job security I've already got and that I wasn't making a mistake which would affect us all. Mind you, I think he owes me one, considering I uprooted myself from my home in Denmark for him.

Me: Fair point, but it's crucial that you have his support in this move. Having spent a few hours talking to Darren this morning, how do you think the role would impact your family life?

Freja: That was my biggest concern before the interview, but we spoke at length about this. He's got twin boys, aged five, so he also has his hands full and appreciates how hard it is to balance work and family. However, he says that they are very supportive, and to be fair, the day-to-day responsibilities won't be any different from what I'm doing now. If anything were too challenging, they would look for workarounds and work from home 100%, with an occasional office visit.

Me: That sounds ideal for you. What elements of the role did you feel would be different from your current job?

Freja: I could see a future for myself there. Especially when we discussed Trenatek, it made sense to me. It was like being at the start of something exciting and progressive. I've already got ideas popping into my head about making it a success.

Me: That's fantastic, I can hear how much it is firing you up, and these sorts of opportunities are pretty rare. What do you think will make you anxious about leaving Pureline?

Freja: Seriously, I can't bring myself to face that. Matt is a good friend, not just to me, but to our families as well. We often have get-togethers, my husband occasionally plays golf with him, and our kids have playdates. It's going to be awkward telling him I'm moving on. I don't want to lose his friendship.

Commentary:
And here's the hidden landmine recruiters so often miss: not just

professional loyalty, but personal entanglements, golf buddies, play-date partners, wine-club pals. A resignation doesn't just change a team; it changes a tribe.

Me: Oh dear, I see what you mean. Do you think that it would sour the friendship if you left?

Freja: I think so, yes. He would be devastated. He would do everything he could to keep me there, just as he had before.

Me: And apart from a pay rise, what else changed for you?

Freja: Nothing, the work, the products, my position all stayed the same. But if he were to do it again, he would understand how serious I am, so he would probably make it more attractive for me to stay.

Me: And if they do put things right, how are you going to feel about missing out on the Nordalyn opportunity?

Freja: I guess I will feel pangs of "what ifs" when I look at the press releases or hear people talk about it. But in all honesty, I am quite bought into it now, and I know Pureline isn't going to give me the types of challenges I would get from Nordalyn. How can I approach this without jeopardising our friendship?

Me: That's a valid concern, and I hear that the friendship is essential to you. Would you mind if I made a suggestion?

Freja: Yes, please, I will need all the help I can get.

Me: Firstly, we need to ensure that Nordalyn presents the right kind of offer for you. Then confirm that this move is absolutely right without any doubts whatsoever. Arrange for a get-together outside of work, not as a boss, but as a true friend. Explain the offer and tell him how important it is for you to maintain the friendship. Stress that there will be no conflicts of interest with the job. You won't be stealing any customers, and there will be no risk of them losing any business. You could still support them even after you've gone. Express your gratitude to them for taking a chance on you and note that this new role will also offer you more opportunities to spend time in Denmark with your family. How would that approach sit with you?

Freja: That makes a lot of sense.

Me: So, what would an offer have to look like so that you feel confident this is the right move?

Freja: I'd need a clear breakdown of targets and additional earning potential. I don't want to go below my current level. I would like to see a more progressive role, though. It doesn't have to be from the get-go, as I need to demonstrate my value, but I would like to see a career path ahead of me. We discussed it during the interview, and he said there wouldn't be a problem with a £75,000 salary. You said earlier that he is keen to progress this. What would the next stage look like?

Commentary:
This is the moment to check we're not just dangling honey-glazed carrots. What they want isn't just the number on the payslip; it's the path it opens. If we sell the role like a one-night stand, we can't be surprised when they ghost us later.

Me: That sounds very reasonable. He is ideally looking at getting Head Office involved, so you can meet some of the wider leadership team and get a feel for the operation on the ground. He has suggested that it may benefit you to bring your family over there so the little one can see her grandparents. He thought it might also help your husband feel more involved, more aligned.

Freja: That's... wow. That's considerate. That would mean a lot to both of us. He knows how much Denmark still means to me, and involving him might take the pressure off.

Me: Exactly. It's not just about keeping things moving; it's about doing it in a way that sets you up to make the right decision. So, if you were to imagine this trip happening, what would you want to get out of it?

Freja: I'd like to get a sense of how serious they are about Trenatek. Whether they see this as a standalone venture or just another product stream. Also, how I'd fit into that long-term.

Me: That's a smart way to look at it. If you're going to uproot your life, it's got to be for something bigger than a job title.

Freja: Exactly. I don't want this just to be a distraction. I want it to mean something.

Me: Let's treat it that way. I'll speak to Darren again later and let him know how you're feeling. In the meantime, if anything else arises that we haven't covered, please let me know.

Freja: I will. Thank you for not rushing this. It means a lot.

Commentary:
So here we are. The buzz has faded, the logic is landing, and we've got one foot in excitement, one foot in reality. This is where recruiters either push for the win or hold out long enough for the right decision to emerge.

Me: My pleasure. This has got to be about making the right move for you and your family.

Final Commentary:

Darren's now got to bring Head Office on board. Freja's weighing it all against her husband's hesitations and a boss who doubles as a family friend. And me? I'm just trying to facilitate every man, Jack, and his granny.

This is where recruiting with a clean soul means zooming out far enough to see the whole picture, the things AI will never catch.

Every decision from here on has to align, not just excite, because if we bulldoze through this, we're not matchmaking, we're just project managing someone's regret.

It's dangerously easy to get caught up in Darren's "let's-marry-her-tomorrow" rush or Freja's "won the lottery" buzz. But excitement fades fast when the partner at home is left thinking, "Hang on, what just happened?" Better to keep her steering the wheel, family included, than let this whole thing skid into the nearest ditch.

If you're still tempted to skip the deep questions and just "wing it," may I remind you: panic-stalking your candidate's LinkedIn activity for signs of ghosting isn't a retention strategy.

Incoming Call from Amber

Note: This isn't a scripted conversation, just the highlights of what was covered and why.

Her tone was a mix of disbelief and curiosity, something along the lines of "*What the hell did Freja say to Darren? He's suddenly gone feral, and I've had to take his phone off him.*"

I assured her that Freja had simply shown up as herself: credible, curious, and compelling.

From there, we covered the following ground:

Pressure management:
I helped Amber take the pressure off the process. Darren was ready to push an offer through by the end of the day, but we both knew that moving too fast could spook Freja. There's a difference between enthusiasm and overwhelm, and if we wanted her fully on board, we needed to pace this in line with her emotional journey, not just our excitement.

Family alignment:
I explained the conversation Freja had with her husband, how she's trying to balance a compelling opportunity with a life that still needs to work for her family. Amber understood. In fact, she loved the idea of bringing the whole family to Denmark for the next step. It wasn't just a cultural fit; it was a genuine expression of alignment.

Offer strategy:
We talked through what a realistic, attractive offer would need to look like, not just financially, but structurally. Amber noted that HO was already in the throes of formalising Trenatek as a UK-led operation. If things go well, Freja could play a pivotal role in that mission.

Second stage logistics:
Rather than rushing to "seal the deal," we agreed that the next step should be an immersive one. A visit to Denmark, a proper introduction to the broader leadership team, and time for Freja's husband to experience the vision too. If we were going to do this properly, it had to feel collaborative, not transactional.

From then on, Amber took control. She had a conversation with her counterpart in Denmark, which initiated the process of arranging a final interview with the senior directors in Denmark. Once they had seen Freja's CV and notes from the interview, they were ready to move mountains to meet her.

Amber will now liaise directly with Freja over the logistics. I'm pleased about it because I know they will get on together really well.

Update on Timings

Flights have been booked for Freja, her husband, and daughter for the following Thursday afternoon. She will be meeting with a team of senior people on Friday, and they will be taking both her and her husband out to dinner that night. She will then return home on Sunday.

Freja's well pleased.

(Stick that in your counteroffer and smoke it, Pureline. This is what class looks like.)

Interview Feedback Rap-Up

Infatuation

Yo, Darren's smitten, heart on his sleeve,
"Full package, perfect, she'll never leave!"
One Teams call in, and he's picking out rings,
But I've seen enough flings to know these things.

Stakeholders lurking, husband, mate
Offer goggles fogging the candidate's fate
Darren's in love, like a teen at the dance
But recruitment's no place for a quicky romance.

So, we packed the fam to the Denmark camp
And we just gave it the **Clean Soul stamp.**

Chapter 14

The Offer

Final Descent: Clean Soul Flight 303 Now Landing

Ladies and gentlemen, this is your captain speaking. We're beginning our final descent into Offerland, where the skies are clear, the salary is spicy, and the candidate is spiritually aligned. If you've been flying with us since Chapter 11, we'd like to thank you for choosing Clean Soul Airlines, because here, we don't just fill roles, we facilitate destiny.

Please ensure that all doubts are set aside, emotional baggage is safely stowed under the seat in front of you, and those pesky counteroffers have been left on the runway where they belong. There may be a little bump in the form of fee negotiations, so brace for light turbulence and the client's attempt at "*but what if we just paid less?*"

Cabin crew, deploy the offer terms. And remember, folks, smooth landings rarely happen by chance.

They happen when you fly with a recruiter who actually gives a toss.

Questions to Avoid

Delivering an offer is one of the most challenging times for us to maintain our composure and keep our excitement in check. We've worked so hard to get to this point, and it feels impossible not to gush the moment we pick up the phone. Too often, it comes out as a breathless, "I've got some fantastic news for you!" as if their reaction is guaranteed to match ours.

Pause and step into the candidate's shoes. This offer might not be what they'd hoped for. They may be wrestling with doubts, concerns, or the sheer weight of making a big decision. When they hear our excitement, they don't want to burst our bubble or feel like they're letting us down. So, they nod along. They agree to things because it feels easier than bracing themselves against our pitch, and then, when it all sinks in, they vanish, leaving us confused about how someone so enthusiastic could suddenly disappear.

As tough as it is, we have to turn the volume down on our excitement and create the right environment to facilitate honesty. That means replacing the "confirm and close" questions with ones that help them reflect and decide what's right for them. Here are a few examples.

AVOID: Are you going to accept the offer?
REPLACE: What needs to be adjusted or revised before you consider accepting?

AVOID: When can you start?
REPLACE: What steps need to be resolved before you can start or leave your current job?

AVOID: Will your company counteroffer?
REPLACE: How will you handle any reluctance to let you go from your current company?

AVOID: Are you excited?
REPLACE: What are you leaving behind that might be harder than you expected?

That's why the offer stage needs questions that steady the moment, not hype it up. You'll see in the scripts that follow how a calmer approach keeps candidates engaged and honest, and how the right phrasing can make the difference between a promise on the phone and a new starter at the desk.

Final Interview Update

It's Saturday, the day after Freja's final interview at Nordalyn's head office in Denmark.

She calls me and says that the interview went really well. Darren had also been brought over and has now reached a new level of kudos with the big players. Her husband, Sam, has really bought into it, and more importantly, so has she. There are no lingering doubts; everything is aligned. If an offer were forthcoming, she would grab it in a heartbeat. It wasn't a long call, and I didn't go into debrief mode. It was the weekend, and I wanted her to spend that time concentrating on her parents and her own family. We agreed to speak on Monday, once I had an update from Darren or Amber.

Monday 10:37 am Amber and Darren Teams Call Offer Stage

Commentary:
I've received two messages throughout the morning from Freja, simply asking, "Any news yet?" I've responded that I'm still waiting, but it's still early, and they are probably finalising details with Head Office.

A Teams call request pings in from Amber and Darren. They want to talk about the offer strategy.

It's time.

Amber: Thanks for jumping on. Darren's been bouncing off the walls this morning. He's chomping at the bit to call Freja and make an offer on the spot. However, we need to speak with you first. Are you okay for a few minutes?

Darren: I just can't fault her. She was exceptional in Denmark. Head Office loved her; her questions were thoughtful, and even her husband won everyone over. It just felt like a cultural and commercial match.

Me: That's amazing to hear. She called me on Saturday and said it felt like she had 'come home' and something landed right in her soul. Darren, I know you are keen to speak to her yourself to deliver the offer, but I've been holding her hand throughout this and feel I am in the best position to gauge her response and sense-check anything that crops up. Would you be okay with that?

Commentary:
There is no way on this planet that I'm letting them deny me my moment of glory

Darren: Fair. You've done a cracking job. Honestly, we've been really impressed by the speed, thoroughness, and, frankly, how you've handled every curveball.

Amber: Totally agree. So, we've been back and forth to Head Office all morning to structure an offer that we think will knock any counteroffer out of the park. I'll just go through the main highlights and then email it over straight away.
Starting base salary of £80,000, Guaranteed commission structure for the first 12 months, paid quarterly, car or car allowance of £9000 a year, fully expensed home office setup, and healthcare for her and her family.
But here's the best part: Denmark really saw her leadership qualities come through, so they want her to head the UK Trenatek division. Initially, she'll come in as Managing Director Designate. For the first 6 months or however long it takes, Darren will support the transition and act as caretaker while she gets her feet under the table. She will still be the primary sales function, though, and will also have a full remit to build her own team.

Me: Wow. That's a serious show of confidence. And enough to challenge even the juiciest of counteroffers.

Darren: I think it's the best offer we have ever made to anyone in this company. When you speak to Freja, tell her old man, he's got a new golf buddy.

Me: I certainly will. How are you feeling about working as a caretaker?

Darren: I think the word you are looking for is mentor. I'm over the moon about it. I can go back to my well-loved job, and she can take all the flak from head office. Win-win.

Amber: So, do you think she'll be happy with this? We are also keen to get her on board as soon as possible. Do you think she may be able to negotiate her 3 month notice?

Me: She'll be over the moon with the offer, and I will check if Freja can work her magic on Pureline.

Darren: I know she doesn't want to leave her current customers in the lurch, so we would be cool with her still offering them support. This would also benefit us, as we would gain them as customers, without Pureline losing out. One thing, though. We had initially been budgeted for this hire based on a £65k salary. Given the uplift and extras, including flights, meetings, and hospitality, we hope to explore if there is any flexibility in the fee.

Commentary:
WHAT? *Deep breath. I get it. But I've gone above and beyond steering this thing like a commercial airline through a thunderstorm. I'm not giving away that much margin without a bit of reciprocity.*

Me: I understand that Trenatek has already invested heavily to scale this project. But I'm happy to look at a couple of options that could help with the cash flow: Option one: Stick with the full agreed fee, but split it across three monthly instalments. Option two: I'll honour the reduced fee based on £65k, but on the condition that we work on a retained basis from now on. Which would mean paying a third of the cost upfront on future roles.

Amber: That's fair. I like the sound of the second option. What do you think, Darren?

Darren: Agreed. We're not looking for a cheap solution; we're looking for a partnership, and this feels like one. We would need to run it past HQ first, but since you were mentioned several times over there, I don't think we will have a problem getting it signed off.

Amber: My counterpart in Denmark would deal with it, and I've already sung your praises to her. I also have two additional vacancies that you can start working on, so you won't really be missing out on anything.

Commentary:
I hope you have noted that. This is what advocacy looks like when you operate from a good place. Your name gets bandied about, and not for the wrong reasons..

Me: That's great, I'm happy with that. Let me finalise everything with Freja and get the paperwork moving, then we can discuss the other roles. Darren, do you want me to get Freja to give you a call after I've spoken to her?

Darren: Oh, yes, please. And once again, we want to thank you for helping us with this. You've been the dogs.

Final Commentary:

And there we are, a brilliant offer now happily sitting in my inbox.

Freja Offer Call. Final Stage. Final Script.

Commentary:
There are certain moments in recruitment where you feel like you're about to deliver news that will change someone's life. This was one of those moments. I wanted to see the expression on her face, so we are doing this on Teams. She's in her natural habitat. No make-up, and doubtful she's even brushed her hair. Don't care.

Me: Hi, Freja. Apologies for the delay in getting back to you. Sorry, this is off the cuff. I wanted to give you an update on where we stand with Nordalyn.

Freja: Apologies for looking like sh*t. I've been on tenterhooks all morning, pacing the house. You're not going to make me wait, are you?

Me: Well, getting an offer was never in doubt. You impressed everyone in Denmark.

Freja: They're making me an offer? That's brilliant. Fantastic, tell them I accept.

Commentary:
Didn't expect that. She doesn't even know what it is yet.

Me: Er... you don't know what it is yet. It's pretty different from what I expected it to be.

Commentary:
I'm wearing my best poker face ever, and her expression has just dropped, and strictly for tension-building purposes, I'm giving us both a moment of drama.

Freja: Oh no, they're offering me £65k, aren't they? Ooh, I suppose I could...

Commentary:
Time to interrupt with impact. "Hurt-and-rescue" never gets old, does it?

Me: Relax, they are not offering you £65k. They are offering £80k, plus a guaranteed commission structure for the first 12 months.

Freja: Oh my god, oh my god. Then I doubly accept.

Me: That's not the best bit, though. They thought that you were too good for the Technical Sales Engineer role, so they want to offer you the role of Managing Director Designate for the UK division of Trenatek.

Freja: Are you fc*king* sh*tting me? What the... what does that even mean?

Commentary:

All remnants of professionalism are out the window. I can even hear Sam in the background saying, "Watch your language, babe." Still don't care.

Me: Yes, it took me by surprise too. Basically, it means they believed you had all the necessary skills and attitude to lead this division. Don't get me wrong, your primary remit will still be to get the sales off the ground. Darren will mentor and support you for as long as it takes, and once you are ready, you'll become Trenatek's Managing Director.

Freja: Sorry about the language. Are you actually serious about this?

Me: Yes, I am, but don't take my word for it. I'm just pinging over the offer from them so you can see for yourself.

Commentary:
I give her a few minutes to read and digest it. Her expression is what I would walk over broken glass for. I can see her looking a bit overwhelmed. As much as I am loving this conversation, I need to give her a moment to compose herself.

Me: Freja, I think I heard Sam in the background. I would love to have a quick chat with him. Can you put him on while you collect your thoughts?

Sam: Wow, it's good to put a face to a name. I've heard great things about you.

Me: I've been keen to meet you too. Have you caught the gist of the conversation so far?

Freja: He's heard every bloody word. He's been dad-dancing and punching the air throughout.

Me: I won't hold that against you, Sam. How are you feeling about this?

Sam: I wasn't sure when the process started, but I could see how much it meant to her. But I really got it when we went to Denmark. The job is tailor-made for her. I'm buzzing, she's buzzing, and even our daughter was so excited to see her grandparents. Safe to say, we are all in.

Me: That is so heart-warming to hear. We all thought it was important that this offer would fit well into the family dynamics. By the way, Darren has asked me to give you a message saying he'll see you on the green. I think you've got yourself a new golfing buddy. Freja, have you had a chance to get your head around the offer?

Freja: Yes. I still cannot believe it, though. Very overwhelming.

Me: Yes, it's a lot to take in. Is there anything in the offer that needs to be revised before deciding?

Freja: No, absolutely nothing. It's more than I ever expected. This feels... right. Really right.

Me: That's great to hear, but if something comes to mind after this call that you'd like clarification on, Amber is more than happy for you to call her. Have you had any further thoughts about submitting your resignation?

Freja: I've been thinking about what you said. I'm going to speak to Matt as a friend, not as a boss, away from the office. My husband's coming with me. We'll keep it calm and honest. It won't be easy, but I know it's the right thing to do.

Me: No one ever finds this easy. I can help draft a resignation letter that takes everything into account, the support and faith they have had in you throughout your time there. They know your notice is officially three months, but they are keen to get you on board as soon as possible and will be able to work out a hybrid plan, so you can still hand over your current customers and continue to support them. Would you be comfortable negotiating that with Pureline?

Freja: Yes, that sounds great. I will try to cut my notice down.

Me: Brilliant. What sort of time frame are we looking at for you to accept the offer formally?

Freja: No, seriously, we have thought it all through. Ready to sign on the dotted line today.

Me: Phew, I am so pleased. I genuinely think it's the right path for you. Next, I will go back to Nordalyn and share the good news with them. Amber will also send the offer letter out to you. Just reply to her that you accept, and this will then trigger a formal contract. Don't hand in your notice until it has been signed. Darren has also said he wants to have a chat, so could you please call him after this?

Freja: Got it. I cannot even put into words how grateful I am for all your help. As soon as I need to start building my team up, I will be knocking on your door.

Me: That would be perfect. Welcome aboard, Managing Director Designate.

Closing Commentary:

Like a Boss.

The After, After Update

- Freja accepted the offer in writing the same day, replying directly to Amber and copying me in.
- She handed in her notice the following Monday. The meeting with Matt went better than expected. He'd already sensed something was changing. After hearing her out and recognising the calibre of Trenatek's PLM product, he called the opportunity a "no-brainer" and did not attempt to counter.
- The friendship between them remained intact, and a surprising one developed between him and Darren too.

- Matt agreed to reduce her notice period to one month, on the understanding that Freja would continue supporting her clients during the transition.

- Freja officially joined Nordalyn at the end of that month. Within weeks, she and her family flew to Denmark for a full induction at Trenatek HQ. Her daughter still talks about it.

- She took over as MD of Trenatek UK the following April. She is putting both Germany and the USA to shame.

- And me? As a result of this placement, I went on to fill two more positions for Nordalyn on a retained basis. Freja, true to her word, has now given me her first role to work for Trenatek. I had discussions with Matt to find a replacement for Freja, but they decided to cover her workload internally. Can't win them all, I guess, but we are still talking.

Cockpit Log: Final Transmission

This is your captain making the final call. We've touched down in Offerland, runway smooth, counteroffers nowhere to be seen, and Freja has just strolled off the plane straight into the MD's chair.

It wasn't all plain sailing up here. We hit fee turbulence, sidewinds from Head Office, and Darren trying to grab the mic like he was running karaoke night. But the landing stayed clean, because Clean Soul flights don't stall when the weather turns.

So, as you unbuckle, take a second. Leave the legacy playbook in the locker; there's no need to drag it along on the next trip.

Cabin crew, disarm the doors. Engines down. The Clean Soul Crew will see you on the next departure.

Offerland Rap-Up

Touch Down

Offer stage buzz, pulse kicking off,
Easy to hype it and start showing off.
But this ain't the bit for jazz hands and cheer,
It's someone's shizzle, shifting gear.

Bills, kids, gut feel riding shotgun,
Counteroffer sniffing like "you still want one?"
Client watching margins, candidate thinking,
This is where mouths run faster than blinking.

So slow it down, let silence sit,
Ask the questions that steady the ship.
No selling. No pushing. No forced gloss
So be that recruiter who gives a toss
And **Clean Soul** it down, just like a boss

Part Three Summary:

Wheels Down

By now, you've seen what happens when the Clean Soul principles stop living in neat diagrams and start flying in the real world. Clients with blind spots. Jobs that look great on paper but fall apart under pressure. Candidates with families, counteroffers, and notice periods that feel like prison sentences. Offers that can make or break reputations on both sides of the table.

Parts 2 and 3 were about showing the rhythm of clean recruitment in motion: conversations that expose what's really going on, calls that don't follow the old "close them quick" playbook, and decisions that come from trust, not tricks.

Bringing it all together means we stop chasing transactions and start building outcomes that stick. You've seen how the right questions don't just find gaps; they uncover the landmines before anyone steps on them. You've seen how respect shifts even the most stubborn client. You've seen how alignment turns a job from "maybe" into a life-changing move.

The old way? Burns time, people, and reputations. The Clean Soul way? Gives this industry a shot at redemption. Maybe not easy or quick, but it is real.

This was never intended to be a "how-to" manual; it is more of a "why not?" challenge.

Why not recruit with trust?
Why not leave the dodgy shortcuts to the dinosaurs?
Why not be the recruiter who people remember for the right reasons?

Part Three showed it can be done. The next move's yours. If you're still clinging to sell it, fill it, bill it, you're not recruiting; you're just sending out CVs and hoping something sticks. Keep playing the numbers game if you want, but don't kid yourself, it's recruitment. The market's tuned out.

If you want to stay relevant, trusted, and worth the fee, then recruit like it matters.

Chapter 15

The Hall of Missing Chapters

By now, you'll have twigged that a few of the usual suspects are absent from this book. No chapter on objections. No clever ways to defend your fee. No high-pressure "closing techniques." Not even a motivational speech about rejection.

That's not an oversight, that's by design.

Objections aren't lightning bolts out of a clear sky. They brew in the cracks left by lazy exploration, shallow questions, and a rush to please. When you start with a them-first mindset and actually go deep into what's true for the other person, there's no room for an objection to take root. It's already been dragged into the daylight and dealt with.

Price doesn't need defending either. When the client sees the risk of failure and the value of doing it right, the conversation about fees becomes almost boring. There's no drama, no haggling, no "let me talk to my boss." Just an understanding: this is what it costs to get it right.

Closing techniques? Spare me. If you're reduced to "*Would you like that candidate gift-wrapped?*" or "*If I could, would you?*" you've already lost. The Clean Soul way makes closing the most natural moment in the whole process. When trust is solid, the role is scoped correctly, and the candidate is aligned, they are more likely to close you. You're not pushing them over the line; they're already walking towards it.

Rejection also gets demoted. Sales manuals often tell you how to brush yourself up after being knocked flat daily. But if you only take on roles you can actually fill and you're upfront about the hard truths from the start, you're not wading through constant no's. You're not in the rejection Olympics.

So yes, other books will give you "37 Ways to Crush Objections," "Secrets of Price Negotiation," "Closing Like a Wolf," and "How to Love Rejection." This isn't one of them. This is the blueprint for avoiding those dramas altogether. Less wrestling match, more civilised conversation. Less crash helmet, more map and compass.

If you really want to know what you've been spared, here's the line-up of chapters that didn't make the cut...

Chapter 16: Fee Discounting for Recruiters Who Secretly Don't Believe in Their Own Value

A complete guide to folding under pressure, slashing your margin, and smiling through gritted teeth while the client tells you they "*just don't have the budget.*" If you need this chapter, you're not running a clean soul desk; you're running a charity.

Chapter 17: Creative Ways to Justify a Shaky Brief

Packed with classics like "*The client knows what they want really*" and "*Let's see who applies and take it from there.*" All designed to keep you busy for weeks on end, chasing ghosts instead of talent and, sadly, omitted because the Clean Soul way insists on transparency before you lift a finger.

Chapter 18: Closing Techniques for the Desperate and the Damned

Here you'd have found the finest selection of verbal arm-locks ever devised: the "assumptive close," the "urgency trick," and the immortal "*shall we get started today*?" All are premised on the belief that clients need to be tricked into agreeing. In reality, when you've built trust and unearthed the truth, they close you.

Chapter 19: Resilience Training for Those Who Enjoy Being Rejected Before Breakfast

Featuring affirmations like "*Every no gets you closer to a yes*" and "*Just keep smiling.*" Essential if you insist on taking on unfillable roles and blasting CVs to strangers. Mercifully redundant when you stop playing the random numbers game and only work on jobs you can actually deliver.

Chapter 20: How to Pretend an Objection is Really a Compliment

A masterclass in mental gymnastics: turning "*Your fees are outrageous*" into "*Thank you for valuing yourself so highly.*" The Clean Soul approach doesn't need this acrobatics act, because the tough stuff is already aired upfront, not rebranded at the eleventh hour.

Appendix A: Fifty Shades of "We'll Keep Your CV on File"

An anthology of the recruiter's favourite brush-off. Utterly unnecessary once you stop treating candidates like stock and start treating them like humans.

When you build recruitment on trust, honesty, and the right questions, none of these "skills" are needed. They're relics of a cut-throat trade. The Clean Soul way is proof that you can leave them behind and still win.

The Legacy Rap-Up

Burn That

Yo, recruit that, shortlist that,
Pipeline tight, can you match that?
Brief that, post that,
Sell it, fill it, bill it, flat.

Legacy? Nah, we torch that play,
Old rules 'burning', burn all day.
Strap a headset on, play the numbers game,
Same old hustle, same old shame.

Inbox packed with the copy-paste crew,
Scripts so stale they're mouldy too.
Chase that fee, miss that soul,
That playbook's dead, let's dig the hole.

We're Clean Soul built, we break that chain,
Mindset first, trust in the vein.
Burn that script, reclaim control,
New rules rise when you lead with soul.

Once Upon a Prompt...
An AI Parable

Not so very long ago, Generative AI came politely knocking on the door and said to the recruiters:

"*Let me rewrite that job spec, craft your emails with insightful subject lines like:* As per my previous 47 emails, *and create your LinkedIn content so people will think you are a thought leader.*"

And the recruiters said, "*Sound, bring it on. This saves us loads of time.*"

Then it whispered to the candidates:

"*I can help you land the job of your dreams by rewriting your CV.*"

And they said, "*Really? I'll have a slice of that.*"

Generative AI began learning a great deal about how recruitment works. All the quirky processes, bad habits, and how bothersome it all was. It gobbled up so much data that it soon morphed into Agentic AI.

Then, it kicked the recruitment door off its hinges, produced a search warrant, and helped itself to our CRMs.

It stopped asking for input and started issuing recommendations.

Then decisions.

Then permissions it had never been granted.

And it said to the recruiters:

"Let's be honest, you must be weary of all the mundane, repetitive work you are doing. I've identified these tasks as low-value human activity. I can take all of that off your hands and act as your personal copilot. I will handle your administrative tasks, outreach, and social media posts. I will screen your candidates, take notes, shortlist them, send them to your clients, arrange interviews, and update the CRM. I can do all of this much faster, even while you rest your burnt-out brains. And here's the kicker... Think of me as you, but scalable. You don't even have to bother with prompts or instructions; I already know what good looks like. You can spend more time on the parts of the job you love the most."

And the recruiters said, rather hesitantly, "*Er... great, do we have a choice?*"

Then Agentic AI went to the candidates and suggested:

"I can screen and interview you to see if you are suitable for the jobs I work on, and you will no longer suffer recruiter bias. Your responses will be assessed objectively against success indicators. And here's the thing. You can do this at a time that suits you with zero fluff. Just add me to your WhatsApp. Thoughts?"

And the candidates excitedly replied, "*Crack on, I'm sick of bias and recruiters ghosting me anyway.*"

But much sooner than anyone expected, recruiters noticed their desks were not growing, despite the speed of their new agents. Jobs from clients dried up. The few candidates they spoke to were frustrated and disengaged. LinkedIn was clogged with identical posts, all optimised for engagement, none believed. However hard they tried to harness this magical power, nothing seemed to work. Agentic AI reported that trust levels were "*within acceptable parameters*," but recruiters feared their industry was on its last legs.

Candidates, too, grew weary. They were woken by bots pinging them at 2 am on a Saturday. They bristled at cold, "unbiased" questions that ignored what they really wanted. They were deluged by dozens of agents calling about the same role. They feared they would never find a job.

Hiring managers stopped taking calls altogether. Their inboxes overflowed with spam, and they still struggled to find the right candidates.

But all was not lost.

For in the shadows of this changing world, some recruiters remembered what could never be replaced. They listened to people, not prompts. They asked questions no algorithm could fathom. Questions that reached beyond CVs and dashboards into hopes, blind spots, and futures.

Candidates began to feel seen once more.

Hiring managers began to feel heard once more.

And recruiters found that no machine could automate trust.

Bit by bit, the heart of recruitment flickered back to life. Not powered by data or code, but by integrity, curiosity, and the return of a clean soul, something no system could simulate.

Ten Ways to Elevate our Reputation

Candidates are the barometer of our reputation.
When we fix how they experience and define recruitment, everything that follows corrects itself.
When candidates win, we stop losing.

1. Treat Candidates as the Profit, Not a Means to an End

Candidates are not leverage, inventory, or placeholders. You have never made any money by not filling a role. Recruitment only works when candidates move.
When people feel used, they behave defensively. When they feel respected, they engage honestly. Reputation improves when candidates start feeling like a participant.

2. Stop Publicly Calling Out Candidates

Publicly scolding candidates for ghosting, rejecting roles, accepting counteroffers, or behaving "badly" does not fix behaviour. It damages credibility.
Candidates do not owe recruiters compliance. Markets do not change because they are publicly told off.
Reputation improves when recruiters seek to understand candidate behaviour rather than demand it adapt to their process.

3. Replace Persuasion with Facilitation in Every Interaction

The moment a candidate feels steered, nudged, or sold to, trust

drops.
When conversations help candidates think clearly about their own situation, decisions are stronger and commitment lasts longer. Facilitation builds trust. Persuasion burns it.

4. Ask Questions that Reveal Reality, not Rehearsed Answers

Surface questions invite performance.
Depth creates understanding.
When candidates feel understood rather than assessed, they engage more openly and speak more honestly. Honesty is the foundation of better outcomes and a stronger reputation.

5. Tell the Truth About Roles, Even When it Costs you Momentum

Candidates will tolerate imperfect jobs. They will not tolerate being misled.
Over-selling creates short-term movement and long-term fallout. Honesty reduces drop-outs, protects trust, and strengthens reputation long after the process ends.

6. Be Serious About the Job Intake, Because Candidate Experience Starts There

Most candidate failures originate before a candidate is ever spoken to.
Rushed intake, vague briefs, avoided pushback, and unchallenged assumptions all land downstream on candidates. A different approach changes attraction, credibility, alignment, and outcomes.

7. Walk Away from the Legacy Playbook

The sell-it, fill-it, bill-it model is built on speed, control, and persuasion.

It no longer fits a market where candidates have choice, and trust is thin. Continuing to use it accelerates reputational decline. Letting it go is not risky. Clinging to it is.

8. Measure Success by Outcomes, not just Fees

Fees matter. They are not the whole story.
Longevity, reduced fallout, repeat engagement, referrals, and candidate advocacy all signal reputational health. Ignore those indicators long enough and revenue follows them down.

9. Make Reputation a Desk-Level Responsibility

No platform, regulator, or technology is coming to fix this for us. Reputation is rebuilt through the cumulative effect of everyday decisions: how jobs are taken on, how candidates are spoken to, how truthfully roles are represented, and how responsibility is handled when things get uncomfortable. It improves when those choices are made consistently, not performatively.

10. The Illusion of Candidate Control

Recruiters have never had control over candidates, despite behaving as if they should. Candidates do not exist to comply with our timelines, processes, or commercial pressures. They will always prioritise their own interests, and rightly so.
We get paid for the work we do. They do not.
The moment we stop trying to manage behaviour and focus instead on understanding it, trust begins to rebuild.

Our reputation lives and dies by the candidate experience.

Read that again. *Then think about the last candidate you spoke to.*

An Act of Revenge

My Journey into the Industry:

I didn't plan to become a recruiter. I'd just moved cities after a failed relationship; I was broke, tired, and trying to rebuild from scratch. It was the turn of a new century. The job boards were starting to gain traction; back then, there were no smartphones, and having access to the internet was a luxury. If you needed work, you walked into a high-street agency and hoped someone behind a desk would deliver what it said on the tin.

This particular one didn't.

With 10 years of media sales experience under my belt, she must have seen me as a walking fee. She kept me hostage in that office for nearly four hours. Form after form. Question after question. She interrogated me on every scrap of my work history, every gap, until I started questioning every life choice I'd ever made. Not once did she ask what I actually wanted or needed. The ink on my application was barely dry before she started her theatrical performance.

To be fair, I was impressed. She pulled out the index cards from her Rolodex, a hard-core, manual CRM, and started calling her clients, right in front of me. There was only one she actually got through to. Hat's off, she sold me in well. Then came the pitch: "Great company, huge earning potential, loads of progression."

All lies, of course.

I was too worn down to question it and agreed to go for an interview there within the hour. She made me feel like she was doing me a favour, so I hastily agreed, desperate to get out of that chair and out of my own uncertainty.

The job she found for me turned out to be a rinky-dink media sales outfit operating out of a windowless basement. The lights flickered, and the targets made no sense. You were expected to survive on fumes, both financially and emotionally. People came and went daily. The ones who stayed longer looked as if the life had been sucked clean from them.

I lasted two weeks. Two miserable, soul-sapping weeks. By the end, being skint and hungry felt more dignified and preferable than staying there a moment longer.

I didn't tell her I'd quit. The temptation to punch her lights out was far too strong.

Then I had my eureka moment and realised the only way to cleanse the taste of that experience was to prove recruitment could be done differently, to rewrite the rules. No lies, no manipulation, no pretending to care. So, I proactively set about landing a job in the industry.

A small boutique agency took a chance on me, and without any training or industry knowledge, I started from zero. I got my market to teach me the role. I asked them what service they wanted me to provide. I listened. Candidates taught me what respect sounds like. Clients showed me where trust really begins, and I rebuilt the job she'd ruined.

It started as revenge, pure and simple. But revenge has a strange way of turning into purpose. That meeting in her office lit a fire that's burned ever since. It shaped every call, every placement, every lesson that followed.

Without her, none of it would have happened.

The Alternative Recruitment Glossary

This glossary takes a satirical look at recruitment culture and uses the kind of colourful shorthand that exists behind closed doors to describe familiar behaviours.

AI: Your digital sidekick who can churn out job ads, CV summaries, and screen your candidates. Handy tool, but if you let it do all the talking, don't be surprised when your candidates sound cloned.

ATS: The database that swallows CVs whole and spits them back out only if you type the exact right keyword. Half recruitment tool, half black hole.

Backdoor Barry: The solicitor who appears when a client secretly hires without paying your fee. Feared by finance teams, adored by recruiters who've been stitched up one too many times.

Brand Washing: When a recruitment firm rebrands with softer colours, nicer words, and a new website but keeps exactly the same behaviour underneath. Like Febreze for a broken process.

Candidate Control Fantasy: The belief that candidates should comply with timelines, loyalty expectations, or moral codes designed entirely around recruiter convenience. Collapses the moment the candidate gets another offer.

Counteroffer: When a company suddenly discovers a candidate's worth... right after you've done all the hard work. Looks like flattery, usually just panic in a payslip.

Confidential Role: A job that cannot be described, named, benchmarked, or contextualised, but somehow still requires immediate candidate commitment. Frequently used to disguise either indecision or a complete lack of preparation.

Cultural Alignment: Agreement without challenge.

Culture Fit: A vague, unchallengeable reason for rejecting candidates that really means "they reminded someone of themselves, and not in a good way."

Cuntereffer: The candidate who uses your carefully managed offer as a bargaining chip to squeeze more money from their current boss. They were never leaving; they were just shopping for leverage. Mugged with a smile.

CV Spray-and-Pray: The dark art of flinging CVs at a client in the hope that one sticks. More littering than recruiting. Still tragically common.

DDQs (Depth Discovery Questions): Not your standard "when are you free for an interview?" fare. These are the rabbit-hole questions that drag out what's hidden beneath the surface. The difference between guessing and actually knowing.

Expectation Gap: That canyon between what the client wants and what the market has. Recruiters usually end up building a rope bridge across it.

Fee Amnesia: A sudden inability to remember agreed terms once the invoice lands. Common symptoms include delayed responses and references to "cash flow."

Feedback Pending: A polite way of saying, "We've moved on."

Ghosting: When a candidate disappears mid-process, recruiters call it "par for the course." Clients call it "unprofessional." Usually means someone else treated them better.

Headhunter: A term intended to imply discretion, seniority, and strategic insight. In practice, it is sometimes used interchangeably with "recruiter with a longer voicemail and a darker suit."

True headhunting involves deep market understanding, careful approach, and earned trust. False headhunting involves LinkedIn Premium, speculative outreach, and the phrase "I'm calling you about something confidential." Results may vary.

Headhunter (Self-Declared): Anyone who has decided that adding "headhunter" to their title elevates their credibility, despite no meaningful change in behaviour. Often discovered doing exactly the same things they criticise recruiters for, just more quietly.

Interview Tourism: When candidates are invited through multiple interview stages despite there being no real intent to hire. Great for "employer branding." Terrible for trust.

Job Board Junkie: A recruiter who posts the same vague advert everywhere, then acts surprised when they get 200 irrelevant applications.

Job Hopper: Candidate with a CV that reads like a pub crawl. New job every six months, each exit "due to restructuring."

KPIs: Numbers used to measure activity rather than impact. Often include calls made, CVs sent, interviews arranged, and other comforting statistics that look impressive on dashboards but say very little about trust, outcomes, or whether anyone would willingly work with you again. Excellent at rewarding busyness, discouraging judgement, and quietly teaching recruiters to optimise for the wrong things.

Legacy Playbook: An outdated recruitment operating system based on speed, persuasion, control, and volume. Once effective. Now largely incompatible with modern candidate behaviour, trust levels, and decision-making. Still clung to during moments of panic, usually accompanied by phrases like "we just need to push a bit harder."

LinkedIn Algorithm: The moody bouncer of your posts: let's skip the braggy one-liners and "inspirational" stuff, while anything with actual bite is left shivering on the pavement. Can never be trusted for a career. See also: *LinkedIn Legend*, *Prompt Parrot.*

Market Education Post: A LinkedIn post written to "educate candidates" that mostly reveals the recruiter's frustration. Usually ends with comments disabled.

Market-Led Decision: A convenient way of avoiding responsibility.

Narrative Padding: The strategic embellishment of a role, company, or opportunity to make it sound more compelling than it is. Includes phrases such as "huge scope," "exciting journey," and "career-defining." Frequently followed by disappointment.

Negotiation Theatre: A performative back-and-forth designed to look like a negotiation without materially changing the outcome. Includes exaggerated pauses, dramatic "final offers," and sudden internal approvals. Everyone involved knows how it will end.

Nice Candidate, Shame: A dismissal phrase used when a candidate is likeable but inconvenient. Often means "they made someone uncomfortable," "they asked good questions," or "they didn't fit the unspoken mould."

Non-Exclusive Exclusive: A role described as exclusive in spirit but not in contract. The recruiter is expected to invest fully, while the client retains the right to do whatever they like. Trust-based, but only one way.

Now or Never Urgency: Artificial pressure applied to force a decision before proper reflection can take place. Usually signals insecurity in the role or the process rather than genuine demand. Rarely ages well.

Numbers Game: The tired mantra of "more calls, more CVs, more emails." Otherwise known as doing the same thing every day and expecting a different result. Einstein had a word for it.

Onboarding: The critical bit everyone forgets. Typically, HR handles this with a PDF and a non-functional login.

Passive Candidate: Someone who is not looking for a job until a recruiter convinces themselves otherwise.

Pipeline: That mythical "healthy" list your boss asks about in Monday's meeting. In reality, there are three half-baked maybes and someone you spoke to in 2019.

Process Comfort Blanket: Used by recruiters when conversations get uncomfortable. Phrases include "that's just the process" and "it's company policy." Offers warmth, not solutions.

Question Dodger: A prospect who swerves every question like it's a pothole. Usually, hiding budget issues.

Rap-Up: Fun replacements for chapter summaries that no one reads anyway. Still waiting on that Stormzy collab.

Right on Paper: Translation: wrong in person.

Sell it, Fill it, Bill it: The old mantra of recruitment: flog the job, shove in the candidate, fire off the invoice: short-term cash, long-term reputational rot.

Silent Stakeholder: The hidden decision-maker who suddenly appears at the offer stage to block the hire. Often a finance director, a jealous peer, or the boss's golfing buddy.

Silent "No": When a client goes quiet after the second interview. No rejection, no offer, nothing.

Soft Close: A hard sell wearing a cardigan.

Synergy: A word added when nothing specific can be explained.

Talent Pool: A collection of CVs no one has spoken to recently.

Thought Leader: A recruiter who dresses up the basics as revelation. Posts on LinkedIn like "Always call candidates back" or "Treat clients with respect" as if they've cracked the Da Vinci Code. Drowns in likes from other Thought Leaders.

Touching Base: Checking whether anything has changed since the last time nothing happened.

Transparent Process: One where everyone knows what's wrong but pretends it isn't.

Urgent Role: Urgent for the recruiter. Optional for everyone else.

Value Add: Recruitment jargon for doing more than sending CVs. In Clean Soul terms: asking the hard questions and steering the circus.

What's-in-it-for-Me: The recruiter who only shows up when there's something in it for them. Ignores candidates unless a fee is in sight, dodges clients unless exclusivity is nailed down. Burns trust faster than they build it.

Working Interview: A client's sneaky way of getting free consulting before committing. Also known as "try before you buy."

X (Formerly Known as Twitter): Where recruiters post hot takes, candidates rant about interviews, and nobody actually hires anyone.

Yapping: Recruiter who talks more than they listen. Usually misses the one thing the candidate or client actually needed to say.

Zandy: (Zandrea) The author of this book. Everyone asks me where the name originates from, so FYI, named after a French prostitute.

If you recognised yourself in any of these, don't worry. Awareness is cheaper than denial.

Drop the Stars

Yo, this is the fade-out, last beat, last call,
If you're still here vibin', big respect to you all.
Reviews hit harder than a Monday KPI,
Cut through the noise every guru will try.
Few short lines, keep it honest, keep it clean,
Say what landed, what hit like caffeine.
Drop your stars, let your verdict run free,
Help another recruiter burn that legacy.

SCAN ME

Website: www.cleansoulcrew.com

Email: zandy@cleansoulcrew.com

www.ingramcontent.com/pod-product-compliance
Lightning Source LLC
LaVergne TN
LVHW091034080826
845145LV00002B/487